Serving in Marin

Stories from the Life of a Process Server

Kent Philpott

EVM
Earthen Vessel Media, LLC

Serving in Marin
Stories from the Adventures of a Process Server

All rights reserved
Copyright © 2025 by Kent A. Philpott

Published 2025 by Earthen Vessel Media, LLC
San Rafael, CA 94903
www.earthenvesselmedia.com

Current edition ISBN: 978-1-946794-46-8

Library of Congress Control Number: 2024926033

Cover and Book Design by Katie L. C. Philpott

No part of this publication may be reproduced, stored in a retrieval system, or transmitted in any form or by any means, electronic or mechanical, including photocopying, recording, or by any information retrieval system, without the written permission of the author or publisher, except by a reviewer who wishes to quote brief passages in connection with a review written for inclusion in a magazine, newspaper, internet site, or broadcast.

To Son Vernon, who as a kid tagged along on many serving missions and enlivened the adventures and made excellent observations. He's with me still as Treasurer and Associate Pastor of Miller Avenue Church in Mill Valley. Yes, that's in Marin County.

Contents

Preface	7
Worth the View	9
Hard Knocks of a First-Timer	12
Papers and Justice Served	23
Sydney and Eleanor	30
Where's the 280z?	36
Unlawful Detainers	42
Send Bruno!	52
Wurtzberg Power Company	56
Doing the Devil's Work?	64
Sausalito Dives	68
Two Sad Cases	72
Attila the Hun School of Charm?	81
A Bizarre Twenty Dollars	87
XYZ Towing, Again?	95
Wild West Marin	103
A Change of Pants	109
When Process Serving Becomes Ministerial	119
Very Professional	125
It Goes with the Territory	130
The Evasive Defendant	137
Sooner or Later	146
The Jerk Deserves a Serve	149
Beach and an Easy Serve	152
Feast or Famine	156
Tricks or Treats?	159
Is It Worth Getting Shot?	163
Will the Real Clara Please Stand Up	169
Confident Is Better	173
God Sent Me	176
Good Night, Mr. Knight	183
The View from #4	190

Motorboat to the Door	196
Being Blind	205
Not a Dull Life	212
Is Serving for Misfits?	215
Don't Assault a Process Server	217
Ordinary Life Exposed	222

Preface

Process serving is the business; the era is the early 1980s; the locale is the San Francisco Bay Area, but most of the work is done in now famous Marin County. The author is the process server, a Baptist minister who left the ministry temporarily, as a consequence of a divorce, after fourteen years serving churches. At first, the author found the lowly job of process serving humiliating and embarrassing, not to mention scary. However, as time passed, the author gained confidence and new understandings about himself and life. The author settled into a job he began to thoroughly enjoy. Traveling through the beauties of Marin in his little white Toyota Tercel, he spread joy and happiness to thousands. The minister/server encounters deadbeats, people trapped in terrible fixes, cheats, crooks, evaders and seductive women up and down the streets and mud paths of chic and wealthy Marin.

Others encountered in the stories besides the persons who are served are the business partner, Terry, an old pro and private investigator, Vernon, the server's son, and Lisa, the second wife. Some of the three dozen short episodes are humorous while others have a sad twist to them. All the events are real life events that have happened to real people. There is no continuous thread that runs through the short stories except for the thinking and personality of the server. Occasionally, the server reflects on the realities of life that can only be gathered in a few brief moments when a would-be defendant opens a door and is confronted by a process server.

Chapter 1

Worth the View

Summit Drive in Corte Madera is steep; the twisting, turning street is narrow and pitted. The street is well named; it leads up to the top of one of the highest of Marin's hills, Christmas Tree Hill, as it is known locally, due to the triangle-shaped placement of a whole neighborhood of house lights seen from afar. It is one of dozens of foothills belonging to Mt. Tamalpais.

My Toyota Tercel barely made it up the grade. This was 7:40pm, Thursday, the tenth of December, a cold night with a full moon, or nearly so. The moon shone brightly through a cloudless sky. Peter Giddings, channel 7 weatherman, said we were between storms.

I was working my way to 505 Summit to serve a summons and complaint. The little engine was straining, the tires sometimes slipping on the soft, muddy places in the one lane road. One thing was for sure—I didn't want to come back up that road, so I was hoping hard I'd find the person I needed to serve.

505 was at the very top of the hill, and the only place to park was immediately in front of the garage which was offset from the street about two feet. No other car could have

passed while I was parked there. Though darkness had settled in, and oaks stood everywhere on the hill and about the house, I could see the place was rather new, all wood and, no doubt, in the quarter million-dollar range (multiply by at least a factor of 7–10 for modern 2024 prices). The house could be described as modern earthy, a beautiful rustic upper middle-class mansion that probably had a hot tub and wine cellar.

A girl of about fourteen opened the door with two little ones in pajamas standing behind her. And there was a dog; there was often a dog. The barking started as soon as I'd parked. A German shepherd it looked like to me, and fortunately it was on a deck five or so yards from the front door and me.

The defendant I was looking for wasn't home—the kids' father—and as I talked to the kids, the barking, which had never ceased, grew louder and louder. Having gone unnoticed was a bit of roof overhang between the deck and the front porch. The vicious looking and sounding dog was tiptoeing along it toward me. When I spotted it, there was only a few feet between us.

Everyone always says to remain calm, and in such a situation that was what I did. In defense, I said, "Oh no, the dog!" The fourteen-year-old came to my rescue as if there was nothing at all to be concerned with. "Gertrude, get back on the deck." Abruptly, the animal obeyed, tail between legs, and it never made another sound.

Another trip up Summit Drive was staring me in the face. In that situation, I try to get as much information as I can: "When would he be home? Where did he work?" were the questions I asked. The girl said he was due back in fifteen or twenty minutes.

A decision had to be made. Was she trying to get a stranger off her porch? Was she simply wrong, and he wouldn't be back for an hour or so? What to do?

Because of the Christmas season and the usual slowdown in lawsuits, there was little work, and I needed money badly. I didn't want to drive back up Summit, but I didn't want to waste precious time either. The road won; I decided to wait a while.

Though my car was small, I ended up having to back down the hill to an open space fifty yards or so below. I got out and breathed in the cold, fresh air. The moon was in front of me shining over the Bay. The lights of Richmond, Albany, Berkeley and San Francisco sparkled brilliantly across the water. The land was solid black, the water dark blue, and the sky just a touch lighter than the water. Directly in front of me were the hills that separate Corte Madera from Mill Valley. Tiburon and Belvedere Island extended out into the Bay. All three bridges were visible: the San Rafael-Richmond Bridge to my left, the Bay Bridge slightly to my right, and the red lights on the Golden Gate Bridge towers were just visible over the Marin Headlands.

Moving lights streamed down Waldo Grade opposite Sausalito, and there was a steady flow of traffic headed north along Bridgeway, the street that runs most of the length of that one time sleepy fishing village.

The lighthouse on Alcatraz flashed its warning to me every three seconds, and the shape of the "Rock" was faintly discernable. There wasn't much money being made standing on the hill there, but the beauty of the place was some compensation.

Chapter 2

Hard Knocks of a First-Timer

Most people think of subpoena when they think of legal documents and process servers. Subpoenas, though, are rare; it is the summons and complaint that comprise the bulk of the workload.

The summons is one page: the front contains the court clerk's name, the name of the court, the attorney's name and address, the name of the process, and the defendant. It says, "You've been sued," in two languages in Marin: English and Spanish. On the back of the summons is the proof of service, a copy of which I must fill out as process server and submit to the court after service has been affected. Lying on the proof of service is perjury, a felony. There is always an original summons that is identified by an embossed seal of the county. The proof is usually done on the back of the original summons. The court keeps a copy of the complaint and the original summons, and the proof of service goes with it. And when that stage is reached, the lawyers make ready for negotiations and/or the trial.

The complaint may be brief; the smallest I've seen was three pages. Or the complaint may be lengthy. I had one that weighed five pounds. I like small complaints, so I can fold them up and put them out of sight in my back pocket. In the complaint, the plaintiff gives the reason for the suit, the cause(s) of action. Probably the most common reason is "complaint for money," or it might be "breach of contract," "negligence," "assault and battery," "fraud," etc. These are civil actions, not criminal; the plaintiff isn't looking for a jail sentence; the plaintiff is looking for money.

Myths affect process serving. Many people think they have the option of accepting or rejecting legal papers. Not so. When I hear that, I give a quick smile and set the paper down on the desk or the floor, say "okay" and walk away. The California code of civil procedure talks about "in their presence." That phrase can be broadly interpreted. My job is to identify the person, state that I have a legal paper for them, and that is it. I've done it at a hundred yards, across bodies of water, through doors, and over intercoms. However, I'd been serving papers some time before I knew the ins and outs and the limits.

Some of the students at San Francisco Law School, where I was attending in 1980, made their living process serving, and through one of them I landed a job with Speedy Serve in San Francisco. "Landed" is an exaggeration; it is fairly easy to get on with a process serving firm. Some places run through many servers a day. The qualifications are a desperate need for money, absolute boldness, an ability to remain calm when people are threatening you with grievous bodily harm, and a time of not over twelve seconds in the hundred-yard dash. And you have to be over eighteen years old. This last requirement is the only one the law demands.

Speedy Bob ran Speedy Serve, and he paid four dollars per serve. No one paid lower. The office was on Ninth and Folsom—a cubbyhole with three desks, thick cigarette smoke, and lots of loud voices.

I didn't know anything about process serving. For the last fourteen years, I had been a Baptist minister, quite conservative, and I looked the part. Needlessly, I found later, I had called for an appointment, and I had my best pinstriped Roos/Atkins suit on when I walked in the door of Speedy Serve, carrying a brief case with my five-page résumé in it.

Bob sat in the back; two rather portly women were stationed behind the cluttered desks, and several servers were perched around and about the desks. Phones were ringing, people were shouting and swearing; business was underway.

After making my reason for being there known, I was invited over to Bob's desk. There was no chair for me, so I stood to the side of the desk feeling like a kid in basic training standing before a drill instructor.

"Do you want to see my resume?"

"No. Do you have a car?"

"Oh, yes."

"What kind?"

"Well, right now a pick-up truck, but I'm getting a more economical car soon."

"When?"

"Actually, I don't know."

"Do you have any experience?"

"A little." (A little lie.)

"Okay, I want you here every morning at nine. Right now, one of the girls will show you what to do."

"Thank you, sir; I'll do a good job."

"Sure."

I hung around the office as best I could, trying to make small talk with a couple of servers. No one talked back to me except in a couple of one-word answers. Gradually,

I realized that any work I got would be taken away from them. And it was clear I was overdressed and overqualified, but I wanted legal work and flexible hours. Besides, I was indeed in bad financial shape. I felt sick to my stomach.

Bob and I had talked at nine thirty and after a couple of hours of balancing myself on the corner of the desks, I decided I needed some air. As yet, no one had given me any instructions on anything. The girls at the desks had looked at me, and it seemed I received a disgusted look a time or two. Nervous sweat was running down my sides; it was a sticky hot September day, and there was a ten-dollar ticket on the windshield of my 1964 International pick-up truck when I found it on Folsom Street. I'd forgotten about the meter. Parking was so bad I decided to leave the truck and pink ticket on it just where it was. I wanted to leave my suit coat and tie in the truck but there was no way to lock the thing up.

After a terrible hotdog and coke at the Doggie Diner at Tenth and Mission, I walked back to the seedy offices of Speedy Serve to see if I couldn't get on with it. Evidently, during the short interval I'd been away, everyone had gone to lunch and had returned. Business was under way and in some unknown and subtle way, Bob and the girls made me feel as if I was unforgivably late after my half hour absence.

Courageously, I asked one of the women, "Do you have work for me to do?"

"Yeah. Take this paper and serve it."

"Thank you."

She turned quickly away to the other work, leaving me with a strange collection of papers in my hand. It seemed best not to ask any questions. Out the door, I safely tucked the document into my briefcase. I realized I would have to serve a lot of papers at four dollars a crack, and all I had for the day so far was one. Oh, well, I thought; I'm a beginner and I would have to take things slow at first. Reaching the truck, I took the parking ticket from underneath the wiper blade and placed it in my wallet.

Sitting in my truck, I studied the work sheet that was paper clipped to the summons and complaint that I'd been given to serve; my very first one. Speedy's work sheet told me I had to go to 333 Market Street, the twenty-eighth floor. The defendant was an attorney, a Stuart Fussel.

San Francisco isn't a big city, but it is somewhat confusing to those who don't know it well. I knew, of course, where Market Street was, but as to the cross street, I had no idea at all. The best approach, I figured, was to drive down Mission, take the first left I could, then right on Market and start looking for number 333.

It had to have been Seventh I drove up because I passed the Bus Depot. That part of the City is filled with no left turns and one-way streets, and there is simply no parking anywhere. It is impossible to exaggerate the condition.

The lower part of Market reminded me of Zion National Park or the Grand Canyon. Massive buildings loom tall and glassy, especially the new ones, and 333 Market is a concrete and glass marvel. The street itself was in shadows; the sun, though, was reflected off the building at about the fifteenth floor and up. Somewhere in that crystal palace, my man was waiting for his summons.

First thing was to find a place to park the truck. There was not a space on Market, only temporary parking and little of that. Round and round I went, Beale, First, Front, Mission, back to Market, looking, sweating, swearing, running low on gas, horns honking, motorists taking advantage of my slowness. And I would earn four dollars for the serve. In September of 1980, four dollars wasn't anything.

2 – Hard Knocks of a First-Timer

San Francisco can get away with considerable annoyances, in that part of town anyway, due to the sheer beauty and vibrancy of the streets and the people. I was awe struck, too, despite my trouble. I was loving the City again. If it had been hot and smoggy L.A., no, Mr. Fussel would have to have waited.

It was nearing two o'clock when a space on Mission near Second opened up for me. I searched my pockets for change to feed the meter and found I had none. A meter maid would tag me for sure, so I tried several of the nearby businesses. Must have been policy; no one would change my dollar bill. A polite smile and a "sorry" was all I got.

Four good-sized blocks stretched between me and my objective, making it impossible to risk leaving the truck. With the temperature of my blood near boiling, I ran to a corner bar. The bartender wouldn't give me change either, leaving the solution of buying a beer. For seventy-five cents, I got a draft beer, drank it in five seconds, hustled down the street to the truck to find I had a pink piece of paper under my only wiper blade. A ten-dollar ticket. Herb Caen had been right about the meter maids. There were so many desperate feelings flooding me that I can't begin to describe them. For a moment, I thought about going back to the bar, but there was no relief; I simply put the quarter in the meter and headed for 333 Market Street.

My building was "south of Market," covering everything south of Market from the Bay to the Mission District. The term really did not fit the area any longer, since all the big buildings went up displacing a notorious skid row area. But the "south of Market" slight of mouth persisted.

Elevators are not easy to figure out, and I didn't the first time I faced the fancy ones found in secular cathedrals like 333 Market. I squished into a crowded elevator on the street level and looked to the panel for my floor. It wasn't there. The elevator bank I'd chosen went only up to the seventeenth floor; the bank of elevators across the hall would have gotten me up to floor twenty-eight.

Up to seventeen I went, down to the first level again, across the hall to the other bank, and finally I was on my way. In appearance I looked like the rest of the people in the elevator: insurance, computer people, lawyers, and secretaries. Lots of secretaries. A surge of a sense of inferiority went through me in the elevator for the first time. I'd been a minister for fourteen years with a doctors degree from San Francisco Theological Seminary; now here I was doing the dirty business of serving a legal paper.

That's how I felt then, but my thinking has since changed. The alteration was slow in coming. I had not understood what a low opinion many people had of process servers. It startled me to hear people rank servers with bill collectors, used car salesmen and real estate agents. For months, I would say I was doing "legal work" rather than process serving. No more; I am satisfied being a process server knowing I do the job well. It is an honest job; I'm not the debtor nor am I responsible for the inequalities in our civil justice system. Any work is good if it can be done with honesty and integrity. And I've noticed that the bulk of people filing lawsuits are doing so because they feel they have been wronged, and some have. Many business people depend on collecting debts through the legal process, and the collection of such debts often means the difference between a profit and a loss, even the difference between staying in or going out of business. Still, it is difficult work, because few people like to be confronted with the reality they owe money and can't refuse to pay it.

The elevator door glided back, and I stepped into a spacious hallway. To my left, I could see a sign announcing the law firm for which Fussel worked, and below the sign was a desk with a pretty young receptionist seated behind it..

The time had come, my first attempt to serve a paper and I was nervous and unsure of myself. The girl smiled and said, "May I help you?"

"Yes – Is Mr. Fussel in?"

"I see his light is lit up so he's on the phone. Do you have an appointment?"

"No. I just need to see him." My words were not flowing. I was speaking inordinately slowly and doing some squirming.

"Can I tell him who wants to see him."

"Sure, Kent Philpott."

"He's free now. I'll check with him."

She was sweet and didn't know what I wanted, but I could see it might be difficult to see Fussel. It also became clear that I would have to formulate some ethics of serving. Should I conceal my reason for being at a business from receptionists and secretaries? Should I try to get the person alone? Should I even serve a person a legal paper at their place of employment? There were many uncertainties whirling in my mind. But there was no time for the finer points.

"Mr. Fussel," she said when she had him on the line," There is a Mr. Philpott to see you. He doesn't have an appointment, but says he only needs a minute of your time."

She turned to me. "He wants to know the nature of your business."

At this stage of the game, having worked out my ethics, I have a number of responses, but in that case, I was speechless.

"Could you tell him I just need to see him for a minute?"

"Mr. Fussel is busy with a client now and can't see you."

Almost wearily, I said, "Okay, I'll come back later." I left.

Back down the elevator I went, discouraged, frustrated and intimidated. I couldn't get past the receptionist. There was nothing else to do but drive back to Speedy Serve. It was nearly three o'clock.

Bob wasn't happy when I walked back in with the unserved paper. He lectured me long and hard on the mistakes I'd made and told me I had to go back and try again.

Once again, the tortuous drive back in the traffic, winding through the one-way streets with no left turn signs everywhere, no place to park, circling through the canyons of high rises, finally finding a temporary yellow space, running to 333, the trip up in the elevator, only to have the receptionist tell me Mr. Fussel was out and wouldn't be back till five.

Thinking it over on the way down twenty-eight stories, there seemed only one thing to do, and I did it – back to Speedy Bob's for another lecture. And I got one with an instruction to be waiting for Fussel at five.

I was so discouraged; I didn't know why I didn't quit right there. Fortunately, there was a desire to get Fussel welling up in me. It was hard to know if I had been lied to and/or avoided, but I wanted Fussel.

At five, I was back, seating beside the receptionist's desk, waiting for my man to return. The receptionist, I felt, was looking at me like I was a bit off or something. I just hated having a nice-looking girl thinking I was weird.

Doubts joined me during my vigil. Probably the guy wouldn't be back at all, and it was to be nothing more than a big waste of time. Maybe he'd sue me for something I was doing wrong, or maybe he was a big guy and would punch me out. It was the time slipping by that bothered me most.

However, I was delighted beyond words when the

2 – Hard Knocks of a First-Timer

receptionist informed me that lawyer Fussel had at that moment stepped off the elevator and was walking towards us. The receptionist helped me by introducing Mr. Fussel to me. I asked him if I could talk to him privately. He invited me back to his office.

Once inside, I pulled the summons and complaint from my back pocket and explained what I had. Instead of a negative reaction, he took the paper saying he had been expecting it. He told me he would have taken it earlier if he had known what I'd had.

"Oh well, " I thought as I got back on the elevator, "At least I got the dumb thing served."

Pink fluttered from underneath my lonely wiper blade again for the third time that day. Thirty dollars worth of parking tickets, one dollar bridge fare, seventy-five cents for a beer, a quarter put three times into parking meters, a long drive home in the commute traffic in my eight mile per gallon truck, and I'd made four bucks.

Next morning at nine, Speedy Bob yelled at me for not putting the date on the summons I'd served Fussel. Fussel, as it turned out had called the plaintiff's attorney and complained about the service and had advised that attorney to change process servers due to the error in not dating the summons.

Of course, no one had instructed me, but I was supposed to be experienced. My little white lie had come around to haunt me. With a lot of commotion, another copy of the summons and complaint was found, and I was ordered to re-serve it. The demeaning and humiliating of an ex-minister was picking up steam.

Back I went to 333 Market, up to the twenty-eighth floor. Fussel wasn't in. But he would be. The lovely receptionist got me a cup of coffee while I waited. Two cups, one Fortune magazine and two New Yorker's later, my man once again disembarked form the elevator. I explained my error, which he already knew about and about which I pretended not to know that he knew, apologized, thanked the receptionist and was away once more.

Thank God there wasn't another little pink slip under my wiper blade. If there had been, that might have been the end.

Chapter 3

Papers and Justice Served

My son and I were sitting in the District Attorney's office at the Marin County Civic Center waiting for the wheels of justice to turn when the guy who had attacked me a couple months before walked by.

"That's the guy who did it, Vern."

"That guy?"

"Yeah, that one right there."

As he walked down the hall past the glassed-in receiving room at the DA's office, our eyes met for an instant. The incident unnerved me some. I already had enough to concern myself with on his account. As it was December 22, a few days to Christmas, I felt compassion to the point of wanting to forget the whole thing. Yet, I believed I had to go through with it for my own personal dignity and for the rights and protection of other process servers. Too often, stories of violence inflicted on process servers elicited laughter, not condemnation.

Officer Battaglia was there in the waiting room, too; he was the cop who'd responded that night when I called the San Anselmo police. He was an experienced officer, and Vern was asking him questions about all the paraphernalia that hung from him. If nothing else, I thought, this would be useful exposure for Vern.

It was on Angela Street that runs off Oak Knoll, which runs off Butterfield Road in San Anselmo that the battery had occurred. This was in October after dark, on a warm and beautiful Marin night, and I was about my business.

Small claims papers amount to maybe ten percent of the workload, and the one I had for Bill Sinclair at 137 Angela was from a credit card company, the dollar amount under one hundred bucks. Evidently, Sinclair had taken out a loan, and somewhere along the line, had stopped paying it back. That was my guess anyway. And I never assume anything, trying not to make any judgments. One never really knows.

Usually, small claims papers were easy to serve, especially since they could be subserved on the very first attempt and I had expected no trouble with Bill Sinclair. The would-be defendant was unknown to me, and I thought only about making a quick commission.

The porch light lit up the small concrete entrance of the fifties type stucco house. My little Tercel was parked right in front of the house. The house was well lighted, and I could see the flicker of blue-grey light indicating a television set was on.

I knocked at the door and as I did, I could hear Howard Cosell's voice doing some commentary on the Monday Night Football. The door swung opened a very few seconds after my knock and a big guy with his shirt off asked me what I wanted.

"Are you Bill Sinclair?"

"You got it. What do you want?"

I didn't like the tone he was using, and I became bashful and hesitant.

"Well," I said as I reached into my back pocket for the

pink piece of paper that was the small claims summons. "I have a legal paper for you."

Giving me a pained and angry look, he asked, "Who the hell are you?"

The fight or flight possibility was looming. It led me into a lie, one that has become habit with me now in uncertain situations.

"I'm Jim Ross, but the paper is from a finance company."

As I spoke, he grabbed the paper out of my hand, tearing it a bit. He was openly scowling now, and I stepped back instinctively.

"Get off my property; you're trespassing."

Those were words I often hear, and I always obeyed. I backed up away and off the porch saying, "Sorry, I'm on my way." Surprisingly, he had not sworn at me. That gave some comfort as I figured he wasn't all that mad.

I stepped off into the darkness and headed toward my car. Bill Sinclair had shut the door and gone back inside. It looked like it was all over except for jotting down the basics of the serve on my work sheet.

It was customary to record the description of the person served along with the date and time. Before doing that, I thought I'd make a notation about the manner of the defendant with a statement that I thought the Sheriff's office could use should they serve any other papers on Bill Sinclair.

Sitting in the car, feeling good about making the serve, and earning my nine dollars, I didn't realize I'd made a major mistake. I had written, "H g...." intending to relate the grabbing of the paper out of my hand when a naked arm shot through the open car window and gripped me by the throat. All I saw was the arm; it was something right out of a horror movie. I couldn't talk; I could barely breath.

My hands were pinned down; I was helpless. The only defense I had was to go limp.

Sinclair was yelling into my face, screaming what had to be murderous threats. I was scared to death as it was, and the hot breath laced with beer was especially terrifying.

My tactic, or lack thereof, worked, as he gradually relaxed his grip on my throat and let me go. The transmission was in gear in an instant, the engine was running, and I was off. My heart was beating fast, and I was nearly shaking. I'm not a little guy, and I'm willing to square off if necessary, but the way the attack had occurred left me with a feeling of powerlessness and fear. Typically, however, as I regained my composure, I got angry, not brave, just angry. Reason was also telling me not to go back to 137 Angela and have it out with Sinclair. But I was going to do something.

There was only one recourse. The police. The San Anselmo Police Department was some ways off, located in the downtown section of that town. Probably, I should have driven down there, but I was too upset to do it, so I stopped in at a firehouse on Butterfield by Arroyo Street.

Fire departments are process server's best friends; they can tell you where all the little streets are that are not on the map. Marin is full of little lanes and private roads that aren't on any maps. But the guy at the local firehouse knows every house on every street and will always tell you just how to get there.

In this case, I simply asked to use the phone. Two firemen were busy watching the football game when I walked in, and they stopped long enough to sit me down near a phone and ask me what had happened.

In five minutes, a San Anselmo cop walked through the rear door of the firehouse, Steve Battalgia, a fifteen-year veteran police officer.

He listened to my story and asked me a number of questions. He produced a form and asked me to fill it out and write out a full account of the incident. Finishing that, he explained I had two options. One – I could accompany him back to 137 Angela and make a citizen's arrest based on the charge of battery. He couldn't do it alone because, for an officer to make an arrest on a misdemeanor charge, he has to have seen its commission personally. A felony is different; he would need only probable cause that a felony had been committed and the subject of the arrest had committed the felony in order to make the arrest himself. Simple battery, a harmful touching of the person of another, is only a misdemeanor. Or, two, my report would be submitted to the district attorney's office. It would then be up to the D.A. as to whether Sinclair would be cited or not.

Steve thought the D.A. would prosecute the matter. He urged me to go with option two, since the first plan would have meant calling for at least one other backup and a possible fight with Sinclair. Being somewhat cynical about the justice apparatus, I really wanted to make a citizen's arrest. Even though I hadn't received any real injury, there was something about the viciousness of the attack and the meanness of Sinclair that I felt the matter should not simply dissolve with no satisfaction. But then, I didn't want anyone else to be hurt, so I settled on leaving the situation up to the district attorney.

For weeks nothing happened. Then, in early December, I received a criminal subpoena in the mail. There was a receipt I had to sign and return to the D.A.'s office. I complied, knowing I would have to take the witness stand in court and testify under oath as to what had happened that October night on Angela Street.

Judge Baty of the municipal court heart the case. I had never been in this court before. Sinclair had pleaded not guilty to the battery charge and had waived his right to a jury trial. Judge Baty would decide the issue.

The prosecutor for the district attorney was a Mr. Jones, a good-looking man about thirty years old. We talked briefly outside the courtroom; he hadn't had a chance to read my report, but I noticed he read it during the opening segment of the short trial.

It was: "The People of the State of California versus Bill Sinclair." The prosecution opened the trial by presenting the state's evidence against the defendant. There was not much to it. I was sworn in; Mr. Jones asked me to tell my story, which look less than three minutes. Sinclair, who was acting as his own attorney, had no questions for me.

Then it was Sinclair's turn. He had his girlfriend there, whom he called as his only witness. She did no more than corroborate my story. I was the only one seated in the audience; I was amazed. Apparently they had not rehearsed their parts, or, when faced with the oath and a judge in black robes, the girlfriend had decided to tell the truth. In any case, it couldn't have been better for the prosecution. She testified that she had seen Sinclair at my car window; she could hear him yelling and swearing at me while his head was in the window. It was a poor showing for Sinclair.

Everything should be as easy. Judge Baty gave the verdict: guilty. No probation report was needed, said Mr. Jones. Mr. Sinclair saw no reason why the sentence shouldn't be handed down right then, so it was. The sentence contained three elements. One, a one-year suspended sentence; two, a $250.00 fine; and three, Sinclair had to write a letter of apology to Mr. Philpott. The case was closed. Vern and I shook hands with Steve Battalgia, and off we went to Mill Valley to serve a summons and complaint on a doctor and a storeowner.

Later that evening, I reflected on what Judge Baty said as he delivered his guilty verdict. He said to Mr. Sinclair that I was legitimately doing my business and that a person serving legal papers, like anyone else, enjoyed the protection against unlawful touching—battery. I knew that many people considered process servers fair game, a person somehow responsible for the anger the served person felt. The process server is to the civil process what a cop is to the criminal process, except there is no badge, uniform, or gun for the process server. But they are protected by the justice system they indirectly work for. I was glad to see justice done.

Chapter 4

Sydney and Eleanor

Sidney White was a hard man to find, and sometimes I didn't want to find him. His wife was divorcing him, and it was my job to serve him the family law summons, so the divorce process could begin.

There was no way of knowing if Sidney knew the papers were coming. Attorneys rarely supply much more information other than the name and address. If Sidney knew what was up and was angry at his wife, I could be in trouble. If he didn't know, he might be shocked and crushed or become enraged on the spot, and again, I might be in trouble. Either way, a divorce action involving large sums of money, children, property, and strong emotions poses the possibility of violence. Sidney had money, kids, property, and maybe a hot temper with big muscles.

The first address I received was in San Rafael in the "Canal" area of Novato Street. Sidney was living in an inexpensive apartment after having moved from what was no doubt a much nicer place on Strawberry Point. It was crisis time for Sidney.

The occupant of the Novato Street address knew who Sidney was but told me he no longer lived there. She

4 – Sydney and Eleanor

smelled like lots of cheap white wine.

"Gee, I really need to talk to Sidney. Have you got a phone number for him?"

"That bastard moved out on me. He told me he was going to help me with the rent then moved out on me. He never paid me a cent."

"That's terrible."

"What are you looking for him for? He owe you money? Come on, you can tell me. He really isn't here; come on in and see for yourself."

An experienced process server will tell you it is not wise to go into a person's house and look around or even go in at all. So far, though, I was anonymous and didn't think there would be any harm done in going in.

"Thanks," I said as I feigned timidity and stepped in. Looking about, I was hoping to say something related to the condition of her apartment, but nothing nice was possible.

"I'm sorry Sidney ripped you off."

"Well, what can you expect from a guy you meet in a bar? He was here a couple of weeks. He sure drank a lot."

As best I could figure, Sidney was in his late twenties. The sloppy woman I was talking to was in her mid-fifties. Maybe he had just been hiding out for free or maybe he needed a drinking partner and a warm body at night. People do a lot of things when their world flips upside down on them.

"I sure need to see Sidney. Wish he had let you know where he moved. Hey, how about where he works. Do you know anything about that?"

"Work! Sidney's too drunk to work. No. Forget about that. Are you sure you're not a bill collector?"

"To tell you the truth, I have a legal paper for him. His wife is divorcing him." I thought the woman might think of a couple reasons for telling me where Sidney was, if she did know, and if she knew about the divorce.

"She's dumping him, huh? Good, she sounds like a real bitch. They deserved each other. Anyway, I wish I did know where that bastard was."

It seemed to me I was hearing the truth.

"How'd you like a glass of wine? You know, I'm about out, so if you want some, you know, stay around with me. You'd best go out and get some more."

"Thanks, but I've got to get going. If I had the time, great, but this is a busy day for me. Maybe another time."

"Anytime you get by, I'm always here, but remember to bring something to drink. I'm partial to white wine."

"I'll think about it."

"Do me a favor; if you find him, get the address to me."

"Sure."

Sidney was going to be put on the shelf until a better address could be found. The lawyer who was handling Mrs. White's divorce was notified that Sidney needed finding and the legal paper went into the suspense file.

It was two months before I had another go at Sidney. This time, it was a residence in the backside of Mill Valley, up against a Mt. Tam foothill in a thick redwood grove. The house could not be seen from the narrow road. Only a mailbox with the numbers on it told me I was in the right place. I walked up to the mailbox and looked around for a path or some other indication of where I might fine the house that went with the mailbox. Off to the left, right through a redwood tree grouping was a concrete platform overgrown with weeds and concrete steps angling up. There were sixty-two steps leading straight up to the two-story house tucked into the side of the hill. I made the count on my fourth visit. It was a long drive and a long walk for nine dollars. Already, I had at least two or three hours in on Sidney and not a penny in return. The only consolation I had was the beauty of the area, the majesty of the giant trees I walked beneath, and the strong pleasing scent of the evergreens.

On my first visit, I heard from a neighbor that Sidney was living with a woman named Eleanor, a girlfriend apparently, who owned a cabin on the Russian River where she spent a good deal of the time. Sidney, it was reported, was with her. Sidney, I thought, had a way with women.

Back and forth I went, building up my thigh muscles. Week after week, I kept at it, generally two or three attempts per week. I began to want Sidney. Every time I made an attempt, I wanted him more. Eleanor was never home either; if she had ever been, I would have given the paper to her as a sub-serve. No Eleanor, no Sidney. But it is generally only a matter of time – diligence pays off.

It was a Tuesday morning. From the neighbors, I'd learned that Sidney and Eleanor were at the Russian River cabin and would be home at the end of the weekend. That information had come from the previous Friday. I figured Monday might be too early, but Tuesday might be sweet Tuesday.

Bright and sunny, warm for 10 AM, I hardly noticed the long climb up. Toward the midway point, I caught a glimpse of the house through the trees and saw a light shining in what I knew to be the kitchen. The excitement I felt at the moment is the force that keeps process servers going. It is something akin to the blood lust the true warrior experiences. With almost irrepressible anticipation, I jogged up the last few steps and walked onto the small wood deck that comprised Eleanor's porch.

There was no curtain in the window, and I could see clearly into the well-kept kitchen. In answer to my knock on the glass, a woman about twenty-five entered the kitchen from another part of the house. She was fairly attractive, with black hair and a full round face. Though it was mid-morning, she still wore a bathrobe, a dark brown one, full length.

My fear was that on seeing a stranger, she would retreat, but no, straight to the door and with a smile she opened it and said, "Hello."

"Hi. Is Sidney here?"

"No, are you a friend?" She spoke slowly with a friendly tone to her voice.

"Not actually, but I need to see him."

Surprisingly, she closed the door behind her and stepped out on the porch with me. She looked at me, stretched in a grand kind of way and commented on the beautiful day.

"It really is nice here, isn't it? You live in a great spot."

"I love it here."

"You're Eleanor, right?"

"How do you know?"

"I've been here before, but I was lost so I asked the neighbor just below you where Sidney lived and they said with Eleanor, here."

"Okay."

"Well, is Sidney home?"

There was specialness about the moment. The serve was assured. Even if Sidney were away, Eleanor was going to get it. And I was intrigued with Eleanor. There was a male-female game in the air.

"No, he's in the hospital now. He had an operation this morning."

Nothing to do then, there was no way I would go to the hospital, and nothing could induce me to make another trip back. I pulled the paper out of my back pocket and showed it to Eleanor. She smiled as I explained the legal document and gave her the usual statement about sub-service.

While I was finishing up, she stretched again, untied her bathrobe and let it fall to the deck. And she was naked and beautiful. Still smiling, she asked, "Would you like to come in for a while?"

Yes, I would have liked to have come in for a long while. However, there was something that bothered me. Sidney was being served divorce papers from his wife; he was in the hospital that moment having just undergone surgery that very morning and Eleanor was ready to have a go at a perfect stranger. Men, I know, are supposed to be always ready, but I wasn't ready for that. And I was in between wives, too. Fact is, I was not pleased with Eleanor's lose attitude, knowing how I would have felt had I been Sidney. I had to say no to the lovely, sexy body.

I did it nicely though. "Eleanor, you are very gorgeous." She was standing there in all her glory. "It would be lovely, I know, but for Sidney's sake, here are his divorce papers." Few decisions have been accompanied with more hesitation. Few decisions have been followed by so much regret.

With my work completed, I was gone. Back down the long flight of stairs I went for the last time feeling flushed and warm, ready to hop in my little white car parked up against the branches of a giant redwood and fill out my work sheet. I jotted down the date and time, Eleanor's hair and eye color, her height and weight, her age, and I could have given a far more extensive description of her if I had needed to.

Chapter 5

Where's the 280z?

Some people are extremely difficult to serve. Among the various epitaphs process servers use for those hard-to-find are skips, evaders, and strokers. The first two are obvious; "strokers" refers to being stroked or lied to. Generally, after a dozen or so attempts, the basic procedure is to notify the plaintiff's attorney, and the document will either be returned to the attorney or special efforts may be requested. These special efforts constitute what is called a "stake-out."

There is nothing glamorous about a stakeout, nothing at all. The first one I went on was in Tiburon, waiting for a guy I later discovered was an Italian mobster. I sat and sat in my car, hour after hour at five dollars an hour. Several times, he roared right past me while I was waving my arms for him to stop. He lived in a house with an attached garage, and he simply entered the garage from the house, started the engine, hit the remote-control button for the garage door to open, and sped off. The best I could do was to wait on the street. The last time it happened, I stood shouting and swearing at him, challenging him to stop and fight me. Good thing he didn't take me up on it. I did, however, serve the paper. In my rage, I threw the paper in the street yelling out, "You've been served." Only I and the defendant would know what had actually transpired. And, yes, it was a questionable serve, but I tried it anyway. That happened two years ago, and I wouldn't even think of such a thing now; I was desperate then. Driving home, I fretted some about possible consequences. After all, I did have to sign a proof of serve, and what if I had to testify in court? Rarely does a process server learn of any details beyond the serve, and that was true in this case.

The five bucks an hour I was earning serving the Tiburon resident was not the standard fee. The plaintiff's attorney could not afford the usual twenty-dollar price, and I agreed to a favor for a special attorney client. Five bucks is a deal for a client; twenty bucks is a good job even when I have to split it with my partner. Customarily, I study and read on stakeouts, play some of my tapes, and even do a little writing. Sometimes I also drink a beer.

Even when a significant or even critical case comes along, if a defendant can't be served, the plaintiff's cause of action is moot, and serious injustice may result. One such case involved the sale of a house, and it appeared that the plaintiff, at least on the basis of the complaint, was being cheated by the seller. After a series of attempts to serve, the plaintiff's attorney asked for a stakeout.

The person I hoped to make the defendant lived in the Canal area of San Rafael on Bahia Way. My plan was to wait in the alley behind the condo where the defendant lived and where the carport was located. I had been told that the defendant always used the carport. Easy enough.

People often know when a legal paper is on its way to them. A collector, or credit manager, or store owner, or the person who thinks he or she was wronged, or the attorney, will have called, sent letters, made threats, and even have said in an unguarded moment, "I'm going to sue your ass." All of the above may hinder the service of legal papers. Many times, I've had people tell me, "I could see you coming." A time or two, people have held out their hands and said "Okay, give me the paper," before I had announced who I was and why I was there. Maybe you begin to look like what you are or act like what you are at the critical moment. Though I have pondered the problem, I have come up with no good answer.

When a person is leery, the job becomes much more difficult. All they have to do is to refuse to answer the door. And the defendant I wanted to serve had long neglected to answer the knocks and rings and poundings. No question that he knew what to expect and was acting accordingly. At least, the carport was open and there was a short walk from the carport to the back gate and the defendant would have to use it to get into his house. There would be a five second time frame for me to work with, the time it would take to close a car door and stride a few short steps to the back gate. I figured there would be time enough if I handled the job just right.

Through the week, beginning with Monday, I parked where I could see the carport and could get quickly to anyone opening the door. Not being aware of the defendant's habits, I guessed he would come home at the normal time, five to seven in the evening. "Consequently, I was at my post close to five and did not leave till seven. That figures to forty dollars a day.

Sometimes I walked around a little to get the kinks out. It was early spring, first week of May; the air was warm, and I hated sitting alone doing mostly nothing. From time to time, I'd be questioned by a local resident as to what I was doing. I merely smiled and said I was waiting for a friend. One particular older woman checked me out every time I was there, and I suspect she thought I was up to no good. If a cop had rolled up, it would have been no surprise to me.

Friday came around and I'd gotten nowhere. It crossed my mind that my quarry had been out of town on business all week and would return Friday evening. The attorney had set a two-hundred-and-fifty-dollar limit, which was coming up quickly and with no results to show for the money already expended. I thought I'd try Friday night and Saturday morning. That, I hoped, would surely do it.

Sitting and waiting in my car, I reflected about the life situation of the person for whom I was waiting. I knew he drove a new 280z; he owned the moderately priced condo; he speculated in real estate; he was accused of co-mingling funds, thereby violating a fiduciary trust. He was forty yours old and dressed flashily with silk shirts and gold chains. Perhaps he had gotten caught in the collapse of the real estate market; maybe a divorce had devastated him. There could even have been physical or emotional problems. There is a story, usually two or more, behind every legal paper.

But it was Friday, and I had a little lady to take out, too. Her name, Lisa, and she was flexible. When I told her we needed to sit and wait and watch, she agreed to accompany me on the stakeout. Money had been tight, and I needed to go on a cheap date.

I was not as chintzy as it may seem. I bought a pizza and a six-pack of good beer. So we sat and talked and ate and drank and hugged. After several hours, the pizza was gone, the beer was gone, and it was dark. The air was still warm, the stars twinkled overhead, a really lovely night in Marin. And there was no sign of the car I wanted so badly to see.

The beer was gone – a situation to be rectified. Lisa

suggested I stay put while she drove over to the nearest source of brew. I liked the idea, so off she went. As soon as I climbed out of the car and stood up, I felt a powerful urge to relieve myself. It was dark; there were bushes nearby, and as I have so very often done on the job, I took advantage of my opportunity. I've always feared that one day someone would be home when I had been sure they weren't and would catch me in the act. But again, I got away with it.

In fifteen or so minutes, Lisa was back with another six bottles plus some corn nuts. She only had to go to the Stop-n-Go on Bellam. For another two hours we drank our beer, ate our corn nuts and steamed up the windows. I knew I wasn't paying as much attention as I should have been to the job at hand. Still, all was quiet in the back of the condo. A few cars had pulled in and out, but the stall about which I was concerned stood empty.

About ten o'clock, Lisa was off for some more beer and a bathroom. I sought the bushes out again and I found myself just a bit unsteady on my feet. Nothing serious—just a good warm feeling. The summons and complaint still rested snugly in my back pocket ready to go. I was still in control.

However, another problem was coming into focus. It was ten o'clock, meaning there was one more hour left to serve the paper. Maybe two. I had always gone with the rule that service of legal process had to be done between seven in the morning and eleven in the evening. Once I heard it was six and twelve. Much later, I was told the time of serve had to be "reasonable" largely dependent upon the lifestyle of the person to be served. That's the way process serving is, full of conflicting notions and sometimes outright confusion. And rules varied from jurisdiction to jurisdiction, and translated that means from county to county, or more properly, from judge to judge. I decided to go with eleven o'clock. One more hour.

Lisa came back with more beer. We had the radio going by now, the windows of the car rolled down, a lovely party for two. The only thing we didn't have was a fireplace.

Time slipped by—a lot of time. Around two-thirty in the morning, I woke up. Cold air probably roused me. The radio was going, but all else in the alley was dark and still. I woke Lisa and we both took stock of the situation. The stakeout was definitely over.

Before I turned the key in the ignition, I looked at the stall again. There it was, the 280Z resting comfortably in its place. Even though the job hadn't gone well, I was ready for more stakeout. Saturday morning. But somehow I'd lost the paper. Lisa and I looked all over, but the bushes, under the seats, everywhere. Saturday morning light brought no help.

Monday, when I notified the attorney I needed another copy of the paper, he said he'd send a copy over right away. That paper never did come, and I didn't press it. I guess someone else ended up sitting in that alley waiting for a 280z.

Chapter 6

Unlawful Detainers

An unlawful detainer is perhaps the most unpleasant paper to serve. The plaintiff in an unlawful detainer is usually a landlord who wants a tenant out. The legal document in effect says someone is unlawfully detaining the property of another. It is essentially a breach of contract cause of action. The tenant agrees to certain conditions, like paying rent, etc. and somehow fails to meet the conditions. I have never seen other than a five-day response time for the defendant from the time of personal service. Response time is the time allowed for the defendant to make an answer with the court. It does not mean a person has only five days to move. If personal service is not possible and substitute service is made, the defendant has ten additional days, making it fifteen in all. The writing of an answer is not a simple task for the non-professional, especially if they have but five days to do so. And it costs thirty to forty dollars to file an answer with the court. But time is the critical factor, and time runs from the day of service, assuming personal service occurs, counting holidays and weekends. Lawyers do not often work rapidly in the first place, and even if a person could get one, the attorney would request a considerable sum up-front, and most people facing an unlawful detainer action don't have any money, or they wouldn't be in arrears in their rent.

Then, of course, there is legal aid, community legal services designed for people with no money. However, it takes several days at best to see a paralegal and many more days will elapse before a real live attorney checks over the paralegal's work and makes suggestions. And by that time, the defendant is in default. Default is simple; it means you lose because you have failed to make an answer with the court in the prescribed time.

I used to think it took month to move somebody out. Not in Marin. Supposedly in San Francisco, it can take a while, even up to three months because of the laws that give various rights to renters. In Marin, the court most often acts on the side of the landed gentry and the renter has little protection. No one that I have ever talked to has heard of a successful verdict for a defendant in an unlawful detainer action.

The process is swift and sure. First comes the posting (affixing to the door) of either a three-day or thirty day notice to pay rent or quit. A few times, I've seen a thirty-day notice, but most often it is three days to pay up or get out. When the time period elapses and there has been no movement on either side, the unlawful detainer is filed with the court by the plaintiff. Once I get the document, I must make a minimum of three attempts, at an hour reasonably calculated to find working people home, over a three-day period. If no one is home and the paper is unservable, an order for posting the unlawful detainer is typed up, taken to the courthouse for a judge's signature, filed with the appropriate court, and the paper is then tacked to or posted on the door in question. The defendant in a posting has an additional ten days to make an answer, fifteen in all. If the defendant can't work something out with the landlord after that fifteen-day period or fails to make an answer with the court, they are in default. The plaintiff then has to prepare a writ of execution for eviction, have it filed with the court, take it to the sheriff's office along with a check for the appropriate amount and that's it. The sheriff will post a notice of eviction on the defendant's door saying in a certain number of days, usually about a week, they must be out. When that time elapses, the sheriff will actually, and if necessary, forcefully move people right out on the street and change, or have the landlord change, the locks on the doors. If the defendant's property is still on the property, the sheriff will allow a few more days before the household items are taken away to place unknown. The property can go on the street where looters have free reign.

If a defendant was unservable and gained the longest possible time to answer, fifteen days, the entire process would be about twenty-five days and maybe twenty-two days if the matter were really hustled. However, if the unlawful detainer could be served personally, the whole business could be wrapped up in fifteen days. Out on the street.

Never in my previous fourteen years of being a minister have I seen such tragedy as that associated with unlawful detainers. I'm not a bleeding heart or I could never function as a process server, but I've seen some sad things. Most often there has been an illness preventing a person from working and welfare could not cover all the bills. A person bought food, clothes and medicine rather than pay the rent. Or, as happens regularly, a landlord raises rent beyond the capacity of people to pay the increase. Many people are simply stretched to the limit and any sizeable addition to the budget is impossible. Complicating matters then is the sudden need to move, meaning a person must come up with two months rent, plus, in many instances, a cleaning deposit. Finding inexpensive housing in Marin is not easy. And, a point which comes to reality for only the poorest, if there is no car, a move is very difficult. I have seen people move carryables by bus and leaving larger items behind.

The unlawful detainer lawsuit protects the landlord. One large apartment complex in San Rafael is owned by a very generous and patient man who is reluctant to throw anyone out. On several occasions action was taken only after tenants hadn't paid any rent for a year or more. I never minded serving those. I rent a house, the same one for the last eleven years, and being down three thousand plus dollars is too much.

One Friday morning I was given a five-day unlawful detainer to serve on three young guys living at nice Mr. Johnson's apartment building. Along with the papers was a letter from the attorney giving me a description of the three and information on when I was likely to find them home. They were home most of the time since none of them worked. However, their girlfriends, with whom they lived, worked and they were home in the evenings. There was an additional note concerning the defendants' disposition. They had threatened Johnson and any process server with serious bodily harm if any action were taken against them.

I loved to see that. Clear, undefiled and undisguised threats. At least I knew what to expect.

Trouble was what I expected, but its form could be almost anything. Kids carry guns and knives sometimes and often haven't figured it out that they can go to jail or worse if they use weapons. Blissful ignorance of consequences can be lethal.

My smile is my defense and it nearly always works.

And the smile is genuine as I enjoy meeting people even if it is to give them a legal paper. If the smile and a humble posture are not effective, I run fast. If no other option is open, I will stand my ground. I consider myself an in shape 195 pounder at six feet one, and I've been in a few scuffles. Not dangerous certainly, but I can be formidable if pressed.

That Friday night I stopped by the apartment. As I climbed the stairs, my heartbeat was increasing and the excitement was on me. It was a little shy of ten o'clock, a tad late, and it sounded like there was a party going on. Loud hard rock sounds jammed my ears as soon as I reached the third level where the apartment was. The door was wide open and already there were beer cans and bottles littering the outside hallway. Young and drunk and belligerent; I wasn't pleased to be there.

The thought struck me that Saturday morning might be better, but I didn't want to come back (the sure sign of a good process server). I could have walked right in, but that might have been asking for it, so I stood on the threshold and knocked on the open door. It took several rapping's to attract anyone's attention. And when they did hear, a half dozen kids or so crowded to the door to see what I wanted. It was not looking good.

"What do you want, man?" one terrifying looking kid asked me.

I knew only the bold approach would work now, boldness and my hard look. I set the hard look and read off the three names right off the legal paper in my extra masculine voice.

"I'm looking for Bill, Joe and Steve."

"Yeah." "Yeah." "Yeah." Just like the Beatles. Three "Yeahs." They were all in front of me along with the rest of their mob.

"You guys, I have a legal paper for each of you."

"Get the fuck out of here," one of them said.

"Not until I give you the papers. Here." And I began handing them out identifying each one as I did. They took them. Simple as that.

One big kid, not one of the three, said, "I'm going to beat the crap out of you."

I smiled, "Then you'd get to go to jail, and bail ought to be around two thousand big ones. Not only would you have a criminal record, but you may not win the fight." To my great relief the kid just gave out a gruff belly laugh and didn't say another word.

The job was done, but I stood there sadistically enjoying the scene I'd created. All of a sudden the three to whom I'd given the papers were the center of attention and they were liking it. Here was something legal and adult and they were impressing the girls.

Then the questions started.

"Hey, what do we do now? Do you work for Johnson?"

"No, I don't work for Johnson directly. Johnson's attorney is my client."

"You always go around doing this to people?"

"Come on you guys – you haven't paid a penny's worth of rent in a year. What do you think? It's time to move. Course, you could talk to a lawyer."

I always say, "see a lawyer." That's all I'm supposed to say, but I generally say more if asked. I'm not to give legal advice, but I do.

"Hey, we'll sue the bastard." Everybody's going to sue the bastards.

"For what, letting you stay here for free? You guys have been lucky. Most landlords would have thrown you out after the first month. Johnson seems like a neat guy to me. Anyway, I'm on my way."

"Don't go," one of the girls said, "come in for a beer."

"Okay." It was too late to continue serving so I stayed around for a couple of beers. The kids were high school age or just a bit older. Several at least were high school dropouts, young losers maybe, no jobs. About all they had were old cars, short-fat girlfriends, and beer and grass. They had some superficial bravado, but not much real courage. As I realized the hopelessness they were in, the beer didn't taste so good. It was time to go.

There were three people I had to serve: Randy Trout, James Trout and Bess Trout. The relationships were not clear from a reading of the complaint. This unlawful detainer had arrived in the Friday morning mail (as most do) meaning it could very well be an all-weekend job.

The house in question was in Mill Valley on Homestead Avenue, a big two-story place with a long approach up a twisting drive and considerable grounds. Trees of varying kinds did their best to shield the house from view. Not a light was shining in the house, but to make the visit count, I had to knock on the front door. Maybe it's the Christian in me that prompts me to fulfill the laws.

It seemed I'd seen this house in haunted house movies. The scene was cold and dark, no moon, no stars, a miserable kind of unfriendly night. My knock went unanswered, as I was sure it would, and as my eyes grew accustomed to the darkness, I could see the house was in bad repair with sheets of plywood tacked up over broken windows. Garbage was spilled along the walk and by the front door.

Though no one answered, it seemed I could hear voices. On the right side of the house, in the second story, a kind of blinking light was visible through a curtained window. It was a familiar throbbing light a television set makes. From experience, I could tell it was a black and white set. Someone was home and had either not heard my knock or was hiding.

To get to the part of the house where the tube was playing, I had to go back to the street and approach the far side of the house. The way to the side door staircase was littered with all manner of debris: boxes, sacks of garbage and broken furniture. From the side of the house, it was quite obvious someone was home; even before I got up to the door, I could tell Dallas was playing on the television.

Some time went by before my knock brought some action. A little voice called through the door, "Who is it?" Her thick southern accent surprised me.

Often I use a fake name, and I did this time. "Jim Ross. Is Randy or James home?"

"Are you a friend of theirs?"

"No, not really."

"What do you want?"

It had come down to it quickly. I wanted that door open and the only thing I could think of was to tell the truth.

"Are you Bess? Well, I need to talk with you a minute."

A bolt slid back, and a young woman peered out at me. She was short, cute, about twenty-three years old, and she had a sad face and tired eyes.

"Bess, I've got a legal paper for you." I said gently as possible as I held it out for her to see. The basics of a serve were there for her, but I wanted Randy and James, too, so I thought I'd hold out as long as possible.

She opened the door and asked me to come in. I wasn't expecting that. The room was depressing, a few sticks of old and battered furniture were stuck around, and a small portable black and white television was perched on a wooden box. I hadn't seen rabbit-ear antennae for years.

"I'm afraid I have an unlawful detainer for you from your landlord."

"I thought so. I know he wants me out."

"Are you alone? Who are Randy and James?"

"Randy is my husband, for a while yet and James is his brother. It's just me and my little boy. He's asleep in the other room."

"I sure don't want you to be the only one served. Can you tell me where Randy and James are?"

Randy is living with a new girlfriend. James is somewhere, but I can tell you where they work. They have a hot tub place in San Anselmo. Just go to Pacific Hot Tubs on San Anselmo Avenue."

"Thanks, Bess. What will you do now?"

"I want to stay here. I'm from Rome, Georgia. My daddy died and I used the money he left me to buy this house. Randy and James put in a hot tub for me, and it worked out at first with me and Randy. He was even going to adopt my son. We got married and James lived with us here."

"Are you working at all?"

"The only thing I've done is apply for a job at Thrifty's. I used to manage a drug store in Rome and did okay."

"You're renting this place now? But you bought the house?"

"After Randy and I got married, he had me quit-claim the house to him, then he sold it to our landlord. Part of the deal was that he'd let us rent it. Randy needed the money to go into solar heating and hot tubs. I thought Randy was taking care of everything, but the letters I got after Randy moved out made it plain he never did pay any rent. As soon as the letters started coming, Randy was telling me it was all over and to divorce him."

"Are you going to?"

"I don't want to. I want him to come back to me and live here. But I guess that won't happen. My mom wants me to come back home. If Randy wants me, he'll have to come to Georgia."

"Can you get home?"

"I've got two older brothers, and they say they'll come and get us. And here, look at this."

Bess Trout handed me a manila folder choked full of all manner of bills and notices. Phone bills, months old—Visa, MasterCard, Emporium, Macy's, bunches of bills.

"Bess, you owe all these bills?"

She bowed her head slightly. "I haven't been able to do a thing."

"Have you tried to get any kind of welfare?"

"Oh, I'd never do that."

She cried some; I said I was sorry and walked to the door. Before I closed the door, I told her home might be a good place to be now.

I wanted Randy and James, but I had to wait until Monday. Saturday I'd found the store and looked inside. The Trout brothers were into hot tubs, solar heating and wine by the looks of things. One corner of the storeroom was furnished with a love seat, two small armchairs, and a low table with bottles of wine and wine glasses on it. A comfortable arrangement.

At nine in the morning, Monday, I was there at Pacific Hot Tubs, and I got 'em. Instead of beating a quick retreat, I stood and watched their reactions as they read the summons. After a moment or two, I said, "You're looking at a five-day unlawful detainer."

They both looked at me with mean hard looks. I did the same back, slowly, and deliberately. It was the least I could do.

Chapter 7

Send Bruno!

"We don't want to send Bruno, but if that's what it will take, well, we'll have to do it."
  As soon as I mentioned Bruno's name, my partner, Terry Cuddy, looked at me with a practiced sidelong glance.
  Terry, a real private eye with a license, is far more experienced at the business than I am. He is the only ex-felon ever licensed as a private investigator by the State of California, and it took a special act of the governor. Two years my senior and an inch taller, Terry, with his bushy graying mustache, long sideburns, authentic cowboy clothes and boots, was what members of the Maltese Falcon Society would call "hard-boiled." I could tell he was wondering why I brought up Bruno to whomever it was over the phone.
  "The reason I called," I continued to the party I had on the phone, "is that I didn't want to embarrass you by serving a legal paper at work. If you'd cooperate with me, it'd be easy."
  It is not usually good practice to call a person you are trying to serve, but with a business address and no home address, I did it sometimes. I knew the business was open

normal daytime hours, and since a standard summons and complaint was involved, I could sub-serve it to anyone at the business except the guard dog. Nothing easier. However, the guy I wanted to make a defendant out of was not going to cooperate. In fact, he was threatening to beat the tar out of me if I showed up at his office.

And that's where Bruno came in. Picture Bruno. Big, strong, ruthless, an arm breaker. The name really got the message across.

Bruno would make the serve if necessary and no one fooled with Bruno. And it worked. The guy calmed down and gave in. "Okay, but let me meet you in the parking lot."

Good old Bruno. I made the serve, and my defendant turned out to be a teddy bear—not the hard-core person he sounded like over the phone.

Terry had given birth to Bruno. He was one of the tools of the trade. We do, however, have a picture of Bruno hanging in our office. It is really a picture of Terry in full gentleman style cowboy fashion replete with ten-gallon hat, sunglasses, big pistol strapped to his waist, and a large German Shepherd lying at his feet. Terry looks fierce. The threat of violence is sometimes a part of the business.

Every time I walk up a set of stairs enroute to a doorbell, my heartbeat picks up speed. There is no way to know what to expect. After my knock, I wait in front of the alien door at a house not on my street to talk to a person I've never seen before. And I think of funny things while I stand waiting. Maybe the person deals drugs and thinks I'm a narc, or worse, somebody he stiffed. Maybe a bullet will splinter the wood, or a dog will be unleashed into my face. It's never happened to me, but it's happened.

For a while, I would stand to the side of the door; occasionally I still do, turned sideways rather than facing it. Cautiously I look around the porch or side of the house for shovels, rakes, boards, anything to defend myself against dogs. My worst fear is to have a Doberman pinscher or other trained killer dog come at me.

A dog did give me the scare of my life once. I had a paper for a guy who ran a dog school. The cover letter the attorney had sent with the paper suggested I call first because the dog school was for training guard dogs. On the phone, I was assured by the person I wanted to serve that he would wait for me at the entrance to the mall where the school was located. Problem was, unbeknown to me, there were two ways to approach the front door of the school, one from the main parking lot, and another from a smaller, less used lot. I used the latter and did not find anyone waiting for me. Thinking there would be no problem, I opened the front door of the dog school and took one step across the threshold. Out of the corner of my right eye, I picked up a rapid, aggressive sort of movement. Instinctively I stepped back and pulled the door with me. In that split second a huge hairy dog slammed into the edge of the door at the level of my throat. From behind me, I heard a command for the dog to stop and in another instant, the guy who was waiting for me had his arm around me asking if I was okay. No question but that I had missed death by the slimmest of margins. It does not seem that serving a legal paper is worth dying for.

A valuable tool of the trade I regularly employ during winter months is a long heavy flashlight. It can show me the way through trees on dark scary nights along narrow paths up the sides of Sausalito or Woodacre hills. My flashlight is good for dogs too. Mostly I use the light to hunt addresses. Thank God for Boy Scout troops and others that paint addresses on curbs. While skips have been known to put up fake numbers, it is easy to detect such a ruse.

7 – Send Bruno!

My map and I go everywhere together. Though I know the county well, streets occasionally turn up with which I am not familiar. I like the Thomas map, more costly than most, but more durable. And no map is always correct. When the map is wrong, it means a lot of wasted time and gas.

No tool is as critical as my car. I easily average one hundred miles a day. On more than one working day, I have piled up three-hundred-plus miles. My little white car takes a real beating. It will be old before I am.

Spending so much time in the car, I need diversions, and my cassette tape deck does it most of the time. I'm a John Denver fan, country western music of all kinds really, and I have stacks of tapes. As I drive around, I often sing along, loudly. People sometimes point and laugh, and when I catch it, I point and laugh back. It is a game I play.

Then, I have the Sum and Substance law series on tape. I'm getting quite a law education as I tour Marin. And this exercise is not lost on my job. I like to read the complaints and understand them, and I can also talk turkey with my clients who are usually lawyers.

This, then, is the real picture of a process server—cruising leisurely about the pleasant hills and bays, listening to good music, growing intellectually, earning fabulous sums of money, and for each mile I travel, I deduct from twenty-five to eleven cents from my gross earnings for tax purposes. I especially like the trips to Berkeley or Walnut Creek or San Francisco or Santa Rosa, where I'm making twenty bucks an hour and thirty cents a mile. Easy money. Not bad for a job that any foolhardy and fearless high school drop-out could do.

Chapter 8

Wurtzberg Power Company

When I worked as an independent contractor for half a dozen different process serving firms, I never got to open the mail. I merely had legal papers with attached work sheets given to me. Rarely did I have the opportunity to read the attorney's cover letters that often contained helpful pointers about the serve. But now, as a real businessman, part owner of a genuine process serving and detective agency, I get to open the mail.

First thing I learned was to open letters without the aid of a letter opener.

"Kent, be careful, will you!" Terry cautioned.

Rip, a telltale sound, and I knew I'd applied too much pressure.

"I told you," Terry continued. "You cut whatever it is in half."

He was right; I'd sawed a summons and complaint up into two pieces.

"Terry, we got any scotch-tape?"

The cover letter was from a Mill Valley attorney we'd never heard of before. A new client—a reason to be glad and a reason to do a good job even to the point of extending extra energy if necessary. Our new client (customer really, but in the legal business, we can get away with client) wanted us to serve a paper on The Pyramid Power and Energy Company of Mill Valley. The name of the prospective defendant sounded like a new age public power utility, but having been around in Marin, we guessed it was some kind of flake organization. The cover letter explained we were to serve the only principle in the company, a Jonathan Segull Wurtzberg at 810 Pine Street in Mill Valley.

"What do you think, Terry?"

"How would I know; you'll just have to see for yourself. I bet though that the place has folded up. See what the complaint says."

The plaintiff was a bank. Wurtzberg, in the name of his company, had run up over forty-five hundred dollars' worth of charges on a visa card. And it was an old account dating back over two years. I noticed further that the complaint had been filed nearly a year before , meaning that Wurtzberg had been evading service. Now it appeared we really did not have a new client at all, but that the lawyer's regular process server could not serve the paper, and we were going to get a shot at it. Of course, we might win the lawyer's business if we were able to serve the paper. The examination of the paper had opened up a number of questions.

A couple of days went by before I got around to trying the paper and it was on a Friday that I thought I'd swing by the Pine Street address on my way into the City. Pine Street is in a section of Mill Valley called Tam Valley. More than likely, the residents in that area don't like it being referred to as a part of Mill Valley. There are two ways to get there. You can take the regular Mill Valley turnoff, go left on Camino Alto off Blithedale, swing around Tamalpais High School, and keep on it until you get to Shoreline Highway at Tam Junction, turn right toward the beach and/or the mountain, and Pine is up a mile or two. Or, if you're smart, you can go past the Mill Valley Blithedale Avenue turnoff until you reach the Stinson Beach turnoff. This turnoff is just past the Richardson Bridge, past Seminary Drive. You stay on Shoreline until you come to Tam Junction and then take a left. I always did it the smart way.

Late winter is generally a nice time in Marin. The floods of 1982 had receded, though there were still a number of roads in Fairfax and vicinity that were closed, but the little pink blooms on some kind of fruit tree were out. The sky was clear, and the air not quite warm. A lovely day.

Pine Street was a familiar street to me, as it was one block away from Laurel, where there is a "stop and rob" store where I often stopped for a cup of coffee. I felt I needed a little caffeine power before playing with pyramid power.

Wurtzberg had decided to make his mark on the world in an unlikely place. His company was housed in a two-story, fifties-style stucco place—a not quite dilapidated, sterile looking building someone had tried to make look like an English country house using one by four redwood boards to outline the corners of the structure and the windows.

No one seemed to be around. I walked all the way around the building, pounding on every door, yelling out "Jonathan" as I went. Newspaper had been taped over the windows, making it impossible to see in. The only sign of life was a yellowed poster, letter size, stapled onto the central door. It announced a meeting conducted by Jonathan Seagull Wurtzberg, director of the Pyramid Power and Energy Company for Friday night at nine o'clock. Who knows how long the notice had been there, yet the meeting offered the only possibility of getting the paper served.

8 – Wurtzberg Power Company

Wonderful, I thought, now I have something to do Friday night.

Typically, I work every day, meaning seven days a week. The alarm gets me going about seven in the morning. I study languages and the Bible, read The Chronicle, eat a little breakfast, and show up at the office at nine. I quit work as close to one in the afternoon as I can. Weekday mornings, I hit all the businesses. Then, in the evening, I head out around six and stop about nine. That's how the process serving sets up; the investigation work, however, is unpredictable.

One of the good things about my job is that I can take people with me. Vernon is my usual companion; he is shotgun. Sometimes it's Lisa, sometimes both; for Wurtzberg, it was Lisa.

We rolled up in front of the Pine Street address ten minutes to nine. The building was dark; the street was dark and quiet except for the light on the corner of Pine and Shoreline Highway. My Tercel was the only car parked in the front of the building. Lisa was sure nothing could be going on, and she was a little upset what we were up to such madness on a Friday night.

Newsprint on the windows didn't do much for the place in broad daylight, and the effect was more startling at night. But the front door was open, and a flickering light could be seen in the interior of the room into which the front door opened. There was an eerie occult sensation in the air.

Lisa and I eased ourselves inside the place a few steps. It wasn't easy getting Lisa in that far, and I'd guess it was only curiosity that made her do it. One lone candle burned dimly at the far end of the room that we'd entered. It was very dark— so dark we had to feel our way along.

There was not another person in the place as far as we knew. Lisa was clutching onto me out of fear. Not a sound hours. The paper was burning a hole in my pocket.

Try as I might, I couldn't think of an appropriate way to break into Wurtzberg's teaching. Of course, he didn't know what was in front of him, so raising my hand was out of the question. I would have to be bold and rude. Somebody was going to be mad at me, Lisa or Wurtzberg. It would have to be the latter.

I whispered to Lisa, "Here I go."

"Good. About time."

The pyramid provided very little illumination and after two steps, I knocked over my first chair. Many others followed like countries in the domino theory. The resulting noise must have sounded like the apocalypse to Wurtzberg. He did stop his rambling lecture to peer out into the semi-darkness.

"Stop it, stop it now. I will not have my sermon interrupted."

"I'm sorry," I offered as I approached him. "Please forgive me – I have to talk to you."

Wurtzberg said nothing. Still gingerly making my way forward, I had the paper out and ready. Sliding chairs out of my way because I couldn't' find an aisle, I felt embarrassed and a little guilty.

"I'm sorry, Mr. Wurtzberg – I have a legal paper for you." I had no class at all.

"Legal paper. You mean you're a damn process server? Well, you dirty bastard, get the hell out of here."

Oh, yes. Those familiar words again.

Wurtzberg started to get up out of his lotus position. Stumbling to the side, he reached out to the edge of the light and made contact with the fabric forming the sides, causing the whole arrangement to come fluttering down, exposing the entire room. It was him and me and Lisa and chairs and the legal paper.

8 – Wurtzberg Power Company

Putting it mildly, he was greatly agitated and was yelling, "Get out of here you son-of-a-bitch. Out. Out of my temple."

"I'm on my way out of your temple. And you're served Wurtzberg – you and your pyramid power company," I said as I laid the paper on the platform at his feet. "I'm gone."

And I was gone. Lisa was already waiting in the car, at the wheel with the engine running.

It was twenty-five minutes to Ignacio after the pizza in Sausalito. We were headed to the Alvarado Inn to hear Tom McNally and company play some of our favorite music, especially J.B.'s electric fiddle. It didn't turn out to be such a bad night after all.

Chapter 9

Doing the Devil's Work?

Saturday morning is my favorite time of the week, and March 5th was a bright sunny one. Driving down Point San Pedro Road toward Peacock Gap, I could smell the salt in the air, as a slight breeze blew in off the bay. Though it was early, there were a number of white sails filled with a westerly wind powering boats across the green water. My usual practice for a Saturday was to attempt service on people I could not get during the week, and if I got to it early enough, people would still be lounging about their homes, not suspecting they were about to be handed a legal paper.

There is something incongruous about a lovely day and process serving. It does not seem so to me now, but in the beginning, it did. Stirring in me that morning was that funny feeling, a sense that there was something not quite right with me. It seemed like a battle to keep going, a heart-and-mind versus necessity struggle. I was many months on the job before I finally came to terms with it; March 5th was yet under the cloud.

First in order was another real estate agent living in a big house, stuck with his investment, maybe purchased when the market was a seller's dream and interest rates manageable. But now, bad times, bankruptcies, businesses closing meant that people who had lived well were trying, oftentimes unsuccessfully, to keep it up. Trying to keep it up not for show so much as hoping to stay afloat and away from moving to Novato or Rohnert Park. The first one was easy, and the guy was even expecting it. He thanked me, too. Great! Off to a good start.

The very next serve was nearby, up on Knight Drive. When I first glanced at the name of the defendant, it struck me that I knew him. The man had been a member of the church I had once pastored. In fact, his whole family had attended. He was an old time Catholic and had gotten involved in the charismatic movement about 1975 and had bolted from his church and joined the congregation where I was. He loved his leisure suits and white plastic belts. And he began hitting it big by selling real estate, about which he "testified" often, saying that it was all a blessing from God, a sign of God's approval.

I knocked timidly on the door. My pulse quickened as I waited for a response. I felt blood rushing to my face – I was embarrassed, maybe even a little ashamed. Here I was, a former pastor serving a legal paper to a former parishioner. After a long moment, I heard the sound of a man's footsteps approaching the door.

"Kent, nice to see you brother."

"Oh hi, Bob – nice to see you, too."

"Come on in, Kent. You know we've prayed for you often."

"Thanks, Bob, but I'm really here on business. Actually, I'm embarrassed about this, but I've got a legal paper for you."

That statement was one of the hardest things I've ever had to say. When Bob had offered his hand to shake, I hesitated for a split second then did it. I wondered if he'd want to take it back.

From nowhere, his wife burst out on me, red-faced, mad and shouting.

"See how you've fallen Kent, doing the devil's work. Satan, be gone. I cast you out of this house of God."

Bob was startled too, I could see, but he was nodding his head in agreement.

"Get out of here; you're trespassing. I rebuke you in the name of Jesus," he said as he began to open the door for me.

A good process server is always ready to fling a paper into an open door. I'd taken the paper out of my back pocket and had it folded twice. I threw it in saying, "Bob, you're served." I felt like adding "in the name of the Lord" but I restrained myself.

And I walked quickly back to my car. Before I reached the street, the Mrs. opened the door and threw the paper out onto the porch.

"We're telling everyone you're working for Satan now. You deserve to be thrown into the pit of hell. Don't ever come around here again."

This time I couldn't resist. "And God bless you, too."

Once again I had to give myself a pep talk. Here were people I'd spent long hours with, working to save their marriage, helping them come to grips with the religious changes they'd experienced. Bob and I had even gone to a Giant's game together. Now I was Satan's emissary. Was I? Should I quit? Was I doing a bad thing? Guilt was working on me. I was well familiar with it. My parents had not given it to me, but I had picked it up in my spiritual pilgrimage. Some of it was helpful and good; most of it was unnatural and harmful. But once it was there, it was hard to get it all straightened out. A dozen times, four dozen times, I'd gone through it, yet I was still vulnerable. Rationally I was secure; emotionally I was divided.

The sunshine made the world bright and cheery; the water in the bay sparkled. Don Williams was singing Miracles on KSAN, and I got hold of myself again. On to the next serve.

Chapter 10

Sausalito Dives

Flynn's Landing in Sausalito is a special place to me, even though I've been there only twice, both times to serve the same bartender. Eddie was friendly and gracious each time – so much so that I stayed to have a beer and talk to a couple of the ladies assembled there.

Sausalito has several good bars and restaurants. The Trident, now gone, was perhaps the best. Horizons is now where the Trident had been with Ondine's for a neighbor in the same building. Scoma's is just north of these two restaurants. Then there is Sally Stanford's Valhalla (but no more Sally), Zack's, Houlihan's, and the finest place in the world for breakfast, Fred's on Bridgeway near Spring Street. Fred's is best on Saturday morning, with strangers sitting at round tables with each other, reading the Chronicle or talking about the flood, jogging, tennis, or cocaine. I usually order eggs and ham, a half order for a very reasonable price. Fred's always gives me a good feeling.

Flynn's Landing is just the place to drink good beer, have a good meal, and meet people. The crowd at Flynn's is older than at Zack's and North Dallas (now gone also, but without regret). North Dallas offered disco type dancing, and the patrons wore a lot of gold with their designer clothes. Zack's attracts locals and San Francisco blacks and Latinos. Flynn's is more my speed—the divorced, easy-going type, thirty to fifty age group. Some serious drinking goes on there among those whose bladders and kidneys can still handle it.

It seemed to me that the women I'd see in Flynn's were almost always sophisticated and attractive and looking for a man. If I didn't have a girlfriend (now, of course, I'm married), I'd be seeing a lot of Flynn's Landing. Naturally, I didn't form all of my impressions of Flynn's from just two visits; some of the ladies I met there filled me in with whispered tones.

San Francisco Bay is nearly as beautiful at night as it is in the day. You can't see the seals and gulls well, but the lights of the City and the surrounding cities of Oakland and Berkeley make it the most gorgeous waterfront scene anywhere. I love the sight of the sailboats with their white sails and multi-colored running lights slipping silently through the cold water. And you can see it all from Flynn's.

At forty, I find I'm still at the stage where I like to act mysterious when I go into places like Flynn's.

The bar was crowded for a Wednesday evening, and there was no place to sit. It was about three deep. Eddie was working hard, and it looked like it was going to be a bit delicate getting him away from the bar to serve him. I sure didn't want to do it in front of everyone, for both our sakes.

For a while, I simply stood at the far end of the bar observing, acting like I was up to something important, insinuating a 'man on a mission' image. Funny looking as I am, I still noticed a lady or two who had an eye on me. One was wearing a man's hat, the kind my father wore when he went out selling Fuller Brush products in the fifties in Portland, Oregon. A soon as I caught her eye, she smiled at me. Oh, the power in a smile. Another lady about her same age, obviously a friend of the lady with the hat and sitting beside her, suddenly stood up and walked away. The lady with the hat motioned for me to come over. My shy smile was subtle and sure.

Dutifully, I took my place next to Sabrina as she said her name was. You'd be surprised at how many Sabrina's there are in Marin. There are a lot of girls named Star, too, and they mostly live in West Marin. There are a few Bodies as well, but they often don't smell too good and are generally unkempt in appearance. These women are usually at least thirty-three now and that's how old I figured this Sabrina was.

A pretty blonde, tall, not too thin, unique in that she'd given up running and tennis. She was into drinking and sex, she said, and proceeded to buy me a couple of beers, excellent dark German beer. When I said I was hungry, she ordered a mixed seafood platter that we shared at the bar. Eddie was still working away and the paper I had for him kept sliding out of my back pocket and landing on the floor under my barstool.

"What the hell is that paper you keep dropping?" Sabrina asked.

"Oh, nothing, just some papers."

"What are you into, porn?"

"No Sabrina, just some stuff from work."

"I'm into porn. Anytime you want to shoot me nude, you can. I love it; we could do it anytime you want."

"Thanks."

"Hey, what do you do?" I guess it was my turn; she'd pretty well told me about herself.

"You don't want to know." It was so much fun to say that.

"Oh, shit, now I know you're into something weird.

What are you, a cop?"

"No, no big deal."

At that moment, Eddie stuck his head in. "I know what this asshole does; he's a damn process server."

Here it was, my cover blown, all the mystery had vanished, and I was presented with a not-too-veiled challenge to fight.

"Eddie, let's go down to the parking lot," I said as coolly as I could. At that point, I was too beer-laden to have done much fighting. Maybe he knew that.

"No, go screw yourself; you probably got another one for me."

"Yeah, I do."

"You may as well give it to me."

With a considerable sense of relief, I realized I was going to get out of a tight squeeze. I handed Eddie the paper across the bar.

"You know this is nothing personal with me. This is my job. I tried to do it the best I could and wait until you left the bar for a break. But you called it, so now it's done."

"Okay man, that's it, you do your job, I do mine."

Sabrina was looking fairly impressed, but the guy sitting right next to me was definitely impressed.

"You're one of those sons-of-a-bitch."

He got to his feet and raised his right arm with a clenched fist at its end. Hopping off the bar stool as rapidly as possible, I hit him hard in the solar plexus with an open palm. Down he went, gasping for breath. So, with Eddie served, Sabrina awestruck, Big Mouth on the floor, and several other Flynn's patrons rousing themselves to the action, I smiled at Sabrina and headed for the door.

Not too bad, really—plenty of good beer, a half-dozen scallops down the hatch, a paper worth twenty bucks personally served, and it was only eleven-thirty. Besides, it had been fun impressing the girls.

Chapter 11

Two Sad Cases

It's definitely rare, but once in a while Terry and I sit around our tiny, even dingy office and chat some with our feet up on our desks and coffee cups in our hands.

Terry always, and I mean always, wears cowboy boots. The rest of his outfit matches the boots. The clothes aren't for effect either. He and his son, Sam, and wife, Sandy, live on a two-acre ranch in Novato with horses, a goat, and some chickens. Terry is a real Marin County cowboy who likes to wear one of his Stetson's while driving his Chrysler Imperial.

When we talk, we mostly talk shop. Sometimes, we talk detective work. Without question, our favorite topic is process serving, which is far and away the more interesting of work-related matters. Somebody generally needs finding or an address is needed, or a way to serve an evader is pondered. Especially after a weekend of serving, there will be several stories worth recounting of what occurred on a serve. Few things are as fun as process serving.

I've never worked less and made more money in my life than I am right now. Currently, Terry and I have reached one income goal and are hoping to pick up the monthly

11 – Two Sad Cases

total to two thousand apiece. It is an attainable goal. Raking it in as we are, we are still on the low end of the Marin scale. Money is not our quest. Time to be and do as we want is what we're after. Time to be with those we love and feel good about our living—that's what we want. And I might say we have more of it now than ever before. I have more peace now than at any other time in my fourteen years as a minister. It has often been said that a minister is to be a servant. I'm still serving.

Occasionally, Terry and I end up doing work for clients we really don't like. We bought the business from a guy who had done process serving for years. When I say we bought the business, I mean we took over his clients, and we inherited one we care very little for. From time to time, I'd notice this particular customer's name in the plaintiff box on the summons, and it often resulted with the serve not going well, or the people served were being ripped off. It happened enough to both Terry and me to make us leery of serving papers for this one client. We had even debated as to whether we would continue taking his business and were in the process of talking about him when he walked into our office.

"Hi Terry. Hi Kent. How are things?"

"Couldn't be better," Terry replied, with somewhat more courtesy in his voice that I expected.

"I got a couple more dead-beats for you to evict out of one of my places. Should be real easy, too, three defendants all together. I was wondering if you'd give me a break on the price?"

Terry was getting interested. "What do you think it would cost you for three defendants?"

"Well, I guess forty dollars. But they live so close to each other you'd be able to do it all in one stop."

"But there are two separate addresses, right? No, you

get the regular rate, twenty bucks a serve. That's how it is for everyone. It could even be sixty, if we end up getting the three at three different times."

"I was hoping to work a deal for thirty dollars for the three of them."

"You going through hard times or something? You're really worried about saving ten or so dollars?" Terry was getting more aggressive. "Look, you know how we charge— take it or leave it."

I would just as soon as have had him leave it, especially since I'd have to do the serving.

"Okay, you can do it. But I sure hope you'll get on it right away. The longer they live in my apartments, the more money they'll beat me out of."

"Don't' worry," I said. "I'll be trying tonight more than likely."

"Well, I hope so."

Of course, if we didn't do the work, someone else would. But that doesn't wash all the time. Someone will do anything. It comes down to making decisions about lawyer's motives and justice in general. Money is always at the heart of it. Someone is going to give some of it up to somebody else. So, it's money and ethics. There is no way to know what is just and what is not from the complaint itself or from the stories you get from either side. Our only means of avoiding the scum is to charge high prices, and we do, the highest in the county. The scums want it done the cheapest way possible. That's been our tactic. Yet, when you're good, maybe the best, the bad sneaks in right along with the rest.

The unlawful detainers were for people living in the same apartment complex on a street in the canal area of San Rafael. The canal is one of my most unfavorite places to visit on a cold and rainy night.

After locating the address and finding a place to park, I dated the summonses, removed the work sheets paper clipped to the legal documents, took off my glasses, folded both papers and put one in my left rear pocket and the other in my right rear pocket. That way, I wouldn't have to return to the car till I'd at least tried to serve both papers.

The apartment building itself was fairly extensive and it took me several false starts before I found one of the numbers. Standing to the side of the door, I gave the doorbell a push. It seemed like the bell didn't work, so I rapped lightly on the door. A little voice answered my knock.

"Who's there?"

"Jim Ross. Is your mommy there?"

Silence for a minute or more.

"Who's there?" a great big voice asked.

"Jim Ross."

"Who's Jim Ross?"

"Just Jim Ross. I have something to give you."

Following that innocent deception, I heard a chain being unhooked and a dead bolt being slid back into the door. Through a tiny crack, a fat face peered out at me.

"I don't know you," the face said.

"Your name is Patricia, right?"

"My name's Pat. How'd you know my name?"

"Actually, your name is here on this legal paper that I have to give to you," I said as I held the paper up for her to see.

She looked at it through the narrow aperture, gave a sign of recognition, and opened the door fully.

A three-hundred-pound blonde and a little brown-headed girl of six or seven filled the doorway.

"I guess you were expecting this," I offered as I gave her the paper.

Big Patricia stood there in a satiny kind of nightgown,

looking grotesque—to me anyway, while the little girl was in her bathrobe. It was six-fifty, dinnertime.

Suddenly she became aware of her condition and abruptly closed the door but asked me to wait. A minute later, the door swung open again and she had changed into a purple-colored robe made out of that terry cloth material.

"Would you come in and tell me what this paper is?"

It is not good practice to enter the house of a person you have just served, but I walked in and sat down on a kitchen chair in her very ill furnished, unkempt apartment. As she looked at the document, I thought about her situation.

Fat, ugly, not too bright, poor, a little daughter, probably no car, on welfare and Medicaid, etc., and now she was being evicted.

She finished going through the paper and asked me, "Do I have to get out now? How long do I have?"

Unnecessarily, I gave her my standard line… "Do you have a lawyer?" Dumb question, but I wanted to be able to say that I had counseled seeing a lawyer, if there was any kind of trouble later on and I would have to testify in court.

"No, I don't have a lawyer."

"Could you afford one, even fifty dollar's worth?"

She laughed.

"Well, you could try legal aid, but you have very little time, only five days to file an answer with the court."

It was hopeless.

"Does this mean I'll have to move?"

"Probably it does. Have you talked to the landlord?"

"Yes, I've been here for years. I hate it here, but I haven't been able to move. He wants me out, because I keep wanting him to fix the stove and the refrigerator, but he won't."

"Do you owe any rent?"

"No, not a penny and I've never been late."

I got up and looked around the kitchen. There wasn't anything in the refrigerator and I could see she was using a one-burner hot plate for a stove. Damn, I wished I were a lawyer so I could try and stick it to the landlord, my client.

"He wants me out," Patricia explained, "because I complain to him."

I guessed so; maybe it was true. After looking through the complaint, I could see no money was owed. She was on a month-by-month agreement, and the landlord didn't need a reason to evict her. He was simply required to give her a thirty-day notice, which he had done. No doubt, she would never see her four-hundred-dollar cleaning deposit again. It would be used to fix the stove and refrigerator. Justice was sure to reign victorious once again.

"Patricia, you have a wonderful little girl there. She is a doll."

"Thank you, Jim. She's all I have."

"How about parents?"

All she said was no to that.

"Patricia, talk to your landlord again. Maybe something can be worked out. But if you have to move, call me. I'll help."

I gave her my card and explained my real name was Kent Philpott. She said she understood the false name, thanked me, and said good-bye as I walked out to the street. It was a tough twenty dollars.

The second unlawful detainer was on the other side of the building from Patricia's place. The apartment complex was built in the shape of a square with a pool and patio in the center. There were two names on the complaint this time: an Ellen and a Hazel.

Within two seconds of my knock, the door flew open,

and I was hit with the smell of a fish dinner wafting in air heated to eighty or so degrees. The smell and the heat suggested old folks and sickness. My heart sank some as I peered into the darkened room that had been opened up to me.

Ellen had to have been a transplanted hillbilly, about sixty, with no teeth and an incredibly wrinkled face. Brown knit pants hung loosely down her skinny legs. Her white top was nearly as wrinkled as the face above but not as clean.

"I don't know a Jim Ross," she stated as I told her who I was. Judging from appearances, I hadn't anticipated her rather authoritative reply.

"I know you don't know me, but I have a legal paper for you. Is Hazel here, too?"

Hazel heard me from somewhere in the interior of the two-bedroom apartment and joined Ellen at the door. And she had a fuller figure to say the least. Ellen did all the talking. I would describe her style of speech as "sad talk."

"I guess it's from the landlord?"

"Yes, I guess it must be."

Ellen took the paper from my hand and examined it. Her toothless mouth was moving like she was working on taffy. Hazel tried to see over Ellen's shoulder.

"They want us out?" Hazel asked matter-of-factly.

"I'm afraid it is what is called an unlawful detainer and means there are some problems," I replied.

Both women stood silently staring at me. There was no hostility in their eyes. I should have walked away, but I remained, out of curiosity.

The silence was broken by a girl in a flannel nightgown who had probably been listening to the entire exchange. She was angry.

"You know why they want us out? Well, I can tell you

mister, it's because of my baby."

She had barged right through the two older ladies and stood right in front of me breathing some kind of horrible aroma right into my nose.

Listening to her style of speech and looking at her face, I was sure she was retarded or somehow mentally deficient. Age wise, she could have been anywhere from fifteen to twenty.

"And it's not fair because of the new law. We're going to fight..."

I liked her right away. Ellen and Hazel started swearing and cussing in an old-time kind of way, thereby giving approval to what the girl was saying.

"I hope you get the bastard," I said, meaning every word of it.

"Damn right," The girl came back as she smiled at me, "Wait, I want to get my baby."

Some little babies are ugly—anyway, they're not cute yet, but this little boy was beautiful. Around four months, I'd say—bright eyed, pink and healthy looking, nicely clothed and wrapped in a baby blue blanket. And the mother, slow of mind from birth perhaps, glowed with proverbial glow. It was real.

"If the landlord wants you out because of the baby, the new law is against him. I hope you have a lawyer to go to."

The young mother was fully animated now. "We don't need one. We know they can't throw us out with my baby. Let 'em try."

For a moment, I considered attempting an explanation of the legal process and urging them to contact a lawyer, but I held my peace. There was such sadness and hopelessness in their situation, that I was intimidated. It seemed like they'd need an army of social workers to get them on their feet.

"Okay, I sincerely hope it works out. If you do have to move, call me. I'll help. Here's my card and my name is really Kent, not Jim Ross. Lots of times I use a different name because you know how mad some people can get. Anyway, call me if you need help."

"Isn't my baby cute?"

"That is the most beautiful baby boy I've ever seen. So long now."

Next morning, I filled Terry in on the serves and ran down the entire story. Terry didn't say much, shook his head a time or two, and that was all. It did occur to me to notify the social services at the civic center and describe the very obvious needs. To the best of my knowledge, a social worker did make a visit on both the households I'd visited the night before. Maybe something good happened, who knows?

Chapter 12

Attila the Hun School of Charm?

Small claims papers can be sub-served on the very first attempt. That's how it is in Marin County, and I believe it is that way throughout California. Neither Terry nor I knew that little fact until one of the lovely ladies at the municipal court told Terry one day.

"How come we never knew this before?" I asked Terry.

I thought of the times I'd gone back and forth to places all over the county unnecessarily, wasting dozens of hours and dozens of gallons of gas. But after that precious ray of light entered our lives, I knew I wasn't going to be walking away from an attempt with that pink sheet at a house where I'd found a warm body over the age of eighteen, even though the actual defendant was not there.

It seemed there could not be anything easier than serving a small claims paper to an accountant during the month of March when that accountant's business address was in hand. If he wasn't at his office, there would likely be a secretary or receptionist, even a janitor to sub.

Soon after the morning's ritual was concluded at our office, I took off on my attempts to serve the businesses. The lion of March was yet roaring loudly that last day of winter, 1981, as the sun was dodging fluffy clouds. Getting out of my car, I had to stand close to it as a school bus full of Drake High School students rolled by with the kids hanging out the windows singing the praises of their basketball teams. Taking the steps two at a time, I bounded confidently up the stairs of the office building on Redhill Drive in San Anselmo, to the second floor looking for suite G. The only thing I had on my mind was how easily this twenty bucks was going to be earned.

Most every time I knock on a door, I feel excitement. I'm often short of breath and I can feel my heart beating. This was slightly different with a surge of energy and expectation; I boldly opened the door to the accountant's office and stepped inside.

"Good morning," I offered to a woman seated behind the desk some seven feet from the front door. I was wearing my big toothy grin.

"Good morning," she returned. She was the picture of the proper secretary with coffee cup in hand, cigarette smoke curling up overhead. Her desk was cluttered, and directly behind her was a sign that read, "A clean desk is the sign of a sick mind." My partner, Terry, has the same slogan pinned to the wall near his desk, right next to the one that says, "Thank you for not breathing while I smoke."

The secretary was about thirty-five years old, a could-be-pretty or once-was-pretty dark-haired woman with a pleasant face and nice smile. I could tell she was a person who liked men and knew how to please them.

"Is Mr. Kolov in?"

"Do you have an appointment?" Right away, I should have been on my guard, but I did not reflect on the wiliness of her reply till later.

"No, but I just need a minute of his time."

The secretary crushed out her cigarette, another sign I

12 – Attila the Hun School of Charm?

missed, stopped smiling and adopted a business-like tone of voice.

"I can't interrupt him. He is with a client now."

She knew what I was there for. Over the years, I've found that if I've got a paper for someone, there may also be other process servers trying to serve other papers. For all I knew, there could have been a stream of them in that office already that morning.

"How long do you think he'll be?"

"At least an hour and a half."

I felt that had to be a lie, though an hour and a half would run up pretty close to noon. However, I was not disturbed since I believed I could just sub-serve the paper on the secretary. But every good process server will try for the personal serve if at all possible. In the corner of the room to my right was a small couch and a coffee table with some magazines on it. Walking over to it, I sat down, smiled again and said I would wait, hoping the accountant would take a break sometime.

The magazines weren't interesting to me: Forbes, Fortune, a couple on real estate, one on computers, all the kinds of reading material I detest, and time was slipping away. I was growing inpatient and thought I might try the bold approach. Pulling the pink paper out and unfolding it, I held it up for viewing.

"I'm going to level with you since you've been so kind to me; I have a legal paper for your boss, Mr. Kolov."

She was not pleased and didn't seem greatly impressed. Surely others had been there before me. Quite firmly, she said, "I can't interrupt him."

It was time to stop being nice. I held the paper up again. "Well, I have to sub-serve you then. The court doesn't care to whom I give it, and you'll do just fine."

Small claims papers are dated, that is, a court date

is fixed for the case to be heard, and that date is stated on the face of the paper. For substitute service to count in Marin County, seventeen days are required from day of service to the court date. I had not thought to check the date on the paper earlier, but I saw it as I held it up. Ten days left, I realized as I did a quick subtraction – time enough for only a personal serve.

For a process server, I had committed a grave sin. My cover was blown. I couldn't give it to the secretary, and I would probably never get by her to ever serve Kolov. In addition, I had to back off my statement about the subserve while at the same time maintaining some kind of posture that would still keep the door open to serve Kolov.

"You know, I've decided not to serve you. I'd really hate to do it to you, so I'll continue to wait for Kolov. Of course, to speed things up and get me out of here, would you please inform Mr. Kolov what I have. The whole thing will just take a few seconds. All I need to do is to hand it to him."

"I could never disturb him."

Oh, brother, what a mess. I was mad at myself and mad at the secretary. She had me. Kolov could have stayed in his office all day. One point in my favor, though, was that I was quite certain Kolov didn't know I was waiting for him. If he did, the secretary was slicker than I thought she was. Yet, there was no way I was going to leave that office; if I failed now, I'd never get it served without a stake-out and no client was going to pay for a stake-out on a small claims paper.

"When will he be free?"

"Not for an hour. I really must get busy, so would you excuse me?"

I refused to answer. I remained seated in the chair, staring down at my feet. Her words suggested she wanted me to leave. To get me out, however, might be noisy and

12 – Attila the Hun School of Charm?

the commotion might bring Kolov out of his office to investigate. She wanted me out, but she wanted it done quietly. I figured I was safe as long as I sat silently. She eyed me with some hostility, and I was indeed embarrassed.

After a tension-filled minute, the secretary went back to her work. Looking around the small office, I saw only a short hallway with two doors leading out from it, one to the left and one to the right. One door was wider than the other and I guessed the smaller door led to the bathroom. Kolov was then behind the other door.

In the uncomfortable silence surrounding the chess game, I could hear voices – two men talking from behind the door that I imagined to be Kolov's. I made up my mind. Standing up, I looked at the secretary, "If I leave now, I'll never get this job done."

Quickly, I stepped into the hall, reached for the door handle, turned it, hoping like crazy it wasn't locked. It wasn't. I opened the door, looked inside and saw my man seated behind his desk.

Glancing at the other man sitting in front of Kolov, no doubt a client of Kolov's, I came directly out with it. "Mr. Kolov, I have a legal paper for you."

Kolov was wild-eyed. "You can't come in. I have a customer here."

True – I hated to do it, and it was tacky, but it was him or me and it was going to be me.

Without saying another word, I stepped up to the desk, placed the pink sheet on the corner of the desk, gave him a big smile, studied him for that brief moment to get his description, turned and strode rapidly out the door.

Blood was rushing to my face; I felt the sweet chill of victory along with the thrill of pending danger.

The secretary was livid. "What is your name? You can't go in there. I'm calling the police."

She did have the phone in her hand. Opening the front door, I looked back to give the woman one last smile. I politely gave her a little wave of the hand, "Thank you for your help. Goodbye now." Down the stairs and I was gone.

At the close of 1981, Herb Caen had a blurb in his Chronicle column about process servers. He does mention our kind occasionally and never favorably. I think Kolov and secretary would have applauded Caen's item. "My greatest discovery: The Attila the Hun School of Charm – a firm of process servers in San Jose."

Chapter 13

A Bizarre Twenty Dollars

"Serve the paper and get out, Kent. Don't stand there and give free legal advice, or compassion either. You're going to screw it up if you do."

The above is sound advice from the guy who taught me process serving. Sometimes I follow it.

One time I didn't do it right was in Sausalito. I had an unlawful detainer for a Robert Kowolski. The plaintiff's attorney had sent a little note along with the paper saying Robert was a photographer and sometime carpenter who was out of work and home most of the time.

Robert lived on Bridgeway right across the street from Scoma's. Parking is difficult in that stretch of Bridgeway, which can cause considerable grief. If you want to turn around and head back north, you must either make a turnabout across the raised divider that runs down the middle of the street and risk a whopping ticket or drive south along Bridgeway until you get to the market on North and Second Streets and figure a way to turn around. This is one of Marin's many messed up driving situations.

I served Robert on the very first attempt. It was easy, the only problem being parking. There was no space on

Bridgeway itself, as it was a Saturday night and Sausalito nightlife was in full swing. One lone parking place on Princess saved me from making loop after loop along the street.

It was the middle of March, raining still, about nine in the evening. The Bay was rough and choppy from what I could see. The City's lights were bouncing off the waves. A large sailboat, looking like a Columbia 50, was anchored seventy or so yards off from the street. A mini storm sent sizable rollers careening off the boat's white hull, and the slap action of the water could be heard faintly.

Robert lived in number ten in the complex of studio apartments. A heavy wire gate barred the entrance, and each apartment had a buzzer and an intercom system set-up. Here it was, the curse of process servers. And there it was, Robert Kowolski, number ten. I didn't want to ring the buzzer because if Robert was in fact home, he'd no doubt come on the intercom with, "Who is it? What do you want? Come back later. Get lost." At least.

A time or two before, when faced with the same circumstance, I've pressed each buzzer, hoping someone would spring the gate for me. This time, I tried the gate and was surprised to find it broken and open. Usually, I would not even glance at the gate, supposing it to be locked and impassable. Maybe out of the corner of my eye, my brain had recorded something I had not previously considered, and my brain just took over and moved my hand. Who knows. But I was in.

Robert's place was one flight up. As I ascended the short set of stairs loud rock music flowed down them and into the entry hall. Climbing the stairs, I folded the legal paper to fit into my back pocket. All I needed to do was to follow the beat to get to the right door. There was a party going on. Before knocking, I listened at the door for a few seconds. The music was so loud I couldn't hear any other sounds.

Parties are not too good to crash if you are a process server. I've done it before, and it's risky. My first occasion to do so was more than a year before the Kowolski serve in West Marin—Bolinas to be exact. It was a hot Saturday afternoon, and I'd driven an hour or so to get to Bolinas and another half-hour had elapsed before I found the house I wanted. The address was at the end of a terrible road on the Bolinas Mesa, there was no street marker, and I had to get out of the car several times to ask directions. The Bolinas Mesa is another world.

"House" is not an accurate term for what I had found; shack is better. Cars were everywhere, beer cans were scattered around, the smell of dope, no doubt home grown, was thick. The people were inside and outside and in cars and on cars. They were drunk, stoned, and other things. Not a few had shed their clothes. It was Bolinas.

My would-be defendant was having a party, and everyone had shown up. It was, in fact, his birthday. This piece of information came my way almost immediately, not more than a few feet from my car. A kid under the age of ten asked me where my present was. After a hem and a haw or two, I asked whose birthday it was and was told. The name matched the one on my legal paper.

For some minutes, I stood around with the paper in my pocket, deciding what to do. It was a long way home and I hated to think about wasting nearly three hours of prime time. I was going to serve the paper regardless.

Surprisingly, I was well received, even though I looked quite different from the others. A completely naked girl came up to me and gave me a kiss full on the lips and asked my name. I gave her my phony one, barely able to get the "Jim" out of my mouth. Just as she was getting more friendly, a guy, also in the buff, grabbed her arm and pulled her away.

As of yet, I didn't know my man by sight, but by questioning a fairly doped out pre-teenager, I learned he was on the grounds somewhere wearing a big Mexican straw hat. The kid said that was all he was wearing. That would certainly narrow the field.

Drinking a beer I'd picked out of a large tub full of ice, I strolled around the place, wove through the shack a couple of times and observed wild goings-on. One bedroom served as an orgy room. It was disgusting actually. Open-minded as I am, it was no place for pre-puberty kids for sure, but some were in there. It was a mellow, fun-loving, perverse group, very hip, and I was feeling just a bit angry.

Anger increases my boldness if I can control it, and my desire to find the birthday boy and get on with it increased. Putting aside my beer, I started asking around. Soon, I had him located. He was extremely drunk and laid out in a wheelbarrow in the front yard. He was nude, as were most of the gang, sprawled out around this king on his throne.

"You're Stevens?" I asked, standing in front of the wheelbarrow.

The straw hat was resting on his face. I had to repeat myself twice more. Still, there was no response. Looking around at the others nearby to see if there was any attention being given me, I noticed that no one was paying any attention. Presently, I reached down and took hold of Stevens' right hand and shook it, hoping to get a reaction. Tugging on the hand, I finally got a response.

"Hey, who the hell are you?"

"I've got a summons and complaint for you. Looks like you're being evicted."

"What?" Stevens was really drunk.

"A legal paper, I've got a legal paper for you. You're being sued."

"Piss on you, man, no one invited you."

"Right. Here's your paper. I couldn't resist opening the document and placing it over his genitals.

Stevens got up quickly then, faster than I thought he'd be able, due to his drunken condition.

"You asshole," he yelled, "get out of here." He raised his right arm to punch me; he swung and missed and stumbled to the ground. For a moment, I was frozen and before I could act, Stevens was back on his feet. I pushed him up straight and laid him back in the wheelbarrow with a soft palm to the chin. And I was off. Out of it as most of the people were, the commotion had begun to attract attention, and I was not far from a real disaster.

If the scene with Stevens had occurred in the backyard, I might have been in serious trouble. But as it was, I had only a few feet to go to get to my car. As I swung my car around in the dirt road, a posse was definitely on its way for me. A couple guys tried to cut me off, but I banged on the horn, gunned the engine and they jumped out of the way. I beat it down the long, pitted road leading away from the mesa, raising a huge cloud of dust behind me. It was a fine way to make thirty dollars.

Bolinas and Sausalito are seemingly far apart; in reality, however, they are quite close.

I banged and banged on Robert Kowalski's door. Suddenly, the music died like a clap of thunder, ominous and threatening. A male voice called through the door, "Who is it?"

"Jim Ross. Hey is Bob home?"

"Sure, I'm him. What do you want?"

"Bob, I need to talk to you for a minute."

"Look, man, can't you hear I'm having a party. It's my birthday."

"Hey, man, happy birthday."

There was a moment's silence. "Okay."
"Ah, yes, " I thought "another twenty bucks."
"Jim, wait a minute. We gotta get dressed here."
Ah yes, I thought, another orgy going on. A full five minutes elapsed. It was a most frustrating five minutes. Giggles and grunts were filtering through the pores in the wooden door.
"Hang on man, we're almost through."
I was sure I knew what "through" meant.
And I had to pee. But there was no place to go and nothing to do but wait.
Just in a nick of time, the door opened. Quickly I stepped inside.
"Thanks for having me in," I said to the guy who let me in. "Are you Bob?"
"I'm Bob," Bob said, "and this is the gang."
The "Gang" was two other guys and four girls, two beautiful black girls and two funny looking white punkers. The punk girls looked fearsome. The guys were early forties, clean-cut doper types with the Clint Eastwood look. Everyone was dressed and stoned with smiles on their faces. There was no scent of grass in the air.
"First things first man, I need a bathroom a minute. I've been drinking coffee all night, and it all wants out at once. Know what I mean?"
"Sure, sure, right down here." Bob took hold of my hand and walked me a few paces toward a tiny hall from whence I could see the bathroom door.
The bathroom was fixed up like a head in a big yacht. Hanging beside the toilet paper dispenser was rack with porn magazines in one shelf and a vibrator and assorted dildoes in the other. There were many other outrageous and art paraphernalia festooning the walls and ceiling.
Walking back from the head, I noticed the whole small

apartment was decorated with unusual artifacts of a deviant nature. Chains and manacles hung from the walls. In the center of the party room, or main room, or whatever it was, was a wooden post. I was beginning to get the picture.

The gang was sizing me up just as I was them. Three guys to do battle with if necessary and the two punk girls looked tougher than Bob and the boys. It was that wooden post I was most worried about though.

"Jim, that's your name, right? You want a beer or some dope? We've got everything here. You aren't a cop, are you?" Bob said.

"No, I'm no cop. Beer, I'd have a beer."

With all eyes on me, I took the beer Bob held out and sat down on a bar stool next to one of the black girls. I smiled at her and asked, "Who are you?"

"My name is Sabrina. And you're Jim. I'm glad you dropped in."

Following our brief introduction, Sabrina began rubbing my upper leg and kissing me, intensely, with a thin long tongue rapidly flicking in and out. In a moment, she stopped and sat back. It was just her way of saying welcome, I guess.

Gradually, I was introduced to the rest. There were no more questions as to what I was there for. I simply sat on the stool and smiled in between gulps of beer.

Loud, extra loud music was playing—not rock music but more like punk or reggae or something in that vein. No one danced, no one talked, everyone just stared and smiled. My guess was that they were spent from the activities that had ended with my arrival and were relaxing between bouts of whatever it was they were up to.

An hour later and another beer or so later, I still had the paper in my pocket. I like to think it was curiosity that made me linger. Yet the music played, and the people sat. Small talk was going on, but that was it. Quite boring really.

Finally, and I mean finally, there was some action. The two punk girls began teasing the black girl who had kissed me. At first, it was talk, then, they were physically pushing and shoving her. Then they began roughly undressing her. I noticed one guy, not Bob, coming out from another room wearing some kind of black briefs, black leather wellington boots, with a mask hand holding a stick my grandmother would have called a switch.

It was time for me to go. Still sitting on the stool, I pulled the summons and complaint from my pocket and called out to Bob.

"Bob. I've got a legal paper for you."

I said it loudly to be heard over the music and I didn't care if the whole bunch heard me.

"What?" Bob responded back.

"A legal paper." And I got up, walked over and put it in his hand.

"Looks like someone wants some money, money you didn't pay them. Thanks for the beer. I'll be going now."

The revelation of my reason for being there didn't upset things much. Black beauty had been stripped and was being tied to the wood post. The rest of the group were shedding their clothes, too. There was no reason to be afraid of an attack because of the legal paper. Rather than fear, I felt sad and sickened. As I walked down to the street, I wondered if I should have done anything or said something. I hadn't done anything; I hadn't said anything. I served my paper. A bizarre twenty dollars.

Chapter 14

XYZ Towing, Again?

Terry does most of the office work, while I run around serving or doing the "field work," as some say. I prefer to use the word "serving." Not that Terry does not serve papers, he does, and he handles Novato exclusively. The workload is divided fairly equally, and the job has run smoothly for nearly two years now. Both of us are quite satisfied.

It is best, I've found, for me to give Terry a chance to settle into the morning a bit before actually saying much more than hello. After struggling through the door with mail stuffed everywhere, he deposits his brief case on the file drawer, finds his coffee cup, then fills it with fresh brewed black stuff, places his body into his black vinyl high-backed chair, swings around, places his boots on the top of his steel blue metal desk, and begins opening the mail. This is all done in complete and reverent silence. If I can be patient, Terry is usually somewhat mellow. The converse can be true.

Sometimes the mail can stir him up.

"Here's another damn paper from XYZ Towing."

I hated to hear that.

"Kent, you want it?"

"No, Terry, I don't want it. I served an S&C on them last week and that was pushing my luck."

XYZ Towing was not an easy serve even when only the corporation was named. The first time I'd been to the business had been a year or so ago when I worked for Marin Process, a company run by a good friend of mine named Jackie Kristenson. Jackie had been a part of my congregation and was a wonderful lady who had stuck by me during the thick and the thin. She'd been in the business four years, and she knew all the dead beats and toughies in the County. Before I went out to serve that first S&C on XYZ Towing, she told me about the people who ran it.

"They'll try to run you off, Kent, and if it looks bad, get out and we'll send the paper to the sheriff. It's not worth it to get beat up."

Thus, I was ready for XYZ Towing. That first time the paper was not for the actual corporation or the owner, a Rod Simon; it was for one of the employees, a mechanic. If the paper had been for the corporation, it would have been considerably easier. But, in that instance, I had to go into the office and ask for the mechanic.

On my first attempt, the company's big and tall blonde secretary told me my man was out sick. The next time, she told me he was on vacation. The third time, I was ready to sub it. After the big blonde told me the guy I wanted was out sick again, I pulled the paper out of my back pocket and gave her the run down about substitute service.

"I'm not accepting anything," she growled in anything but a pleasant manner.

"Fine, you don't have to but here it is," I said as I laid the paper on her desk. "He is served anyway, even if you never give it to him."

"Okay, Okay, I'll call him to the office; he's in the back."

Now I was getting somewhere. There was an intercom system connecting the front office with the back garage. It was a big place, and I could tell there was a lot of activity in the back. In addition to the secretary's voice right in front of me, I could hear her voice blasting on the intercom system as though a trumpet had been sounded in a cave. "John Daly, some damn process server has a subpoena for you. Come in and get it."

Wonderful serve this was going to be, I thought, as I began to get nervous. Like the sensation of a flu bug winning the battle against my body, I had that sickly, weak feeling in my bones.

Quickly the room filled with some of the grungiest looking dudes I'd seen in some time. There were at least eight guys, and I hadn't a clue as to which one was Daly.

"Are you Daly?" I tried on the one standing nearest me. There was no reply at all other than a sever grimace.

"Are you John Daly?" I asked another friendly looking gorilla.

"Hell no, and if I was I wouldn't tell you scum bag."

I smiled at the "scum bag" as it reminded me of my favorite TV show, "Hill Street Blues." It was clear I'd have to take another tack.

"You know, this is just my job like you have jobs. Some people don't like their cars towed away; it always costs money even when they need a tow. Please help me; I need to get this paper to Mr. Daly. I'm just doing my job." I wished like crazy I'd simply subbed the damn paper on the secretary. If I had, I'd be heading north on 101 at that very moment. Now my bones had the flu-like ache in them and sweat was popping out on my forehead.

There was no way for me to know, but Daly hadn't come in yet. And when he did, it was plain he was who he was because he was pounding a ratchet wrench into the palm of his huge hand. It was an extra heavy-duty steel wrench. One tap and bones break.

"Mr. Daly here is your legal paper."

He never said a word, he never stopped with the wrench. "Smash, smash, smash."

"Well, here it is, sir." He was no sir, and I regretted using the word, yet I was anxious for my skin.

Since he wouldn't take it, I knew I'd have to at least drop it on the floor. In doing so, I didn't want it to appear as some kind of defiant gesture, so I bent over slightly and almost laid it on the floor at his feet.

My only hope was to remain calm and confident, though I was anything but. I was so outmatched, it was ridiculous. There was no question but that I would get creamed if I started anything.

I stepped to the door, looked back at the gang and was gone. Walking from the door to my car, I was sure the door would open and I would be attacked. However, I reached the car, opened its door and swung inside. What a safe feeling! The engine was running in one quick second, and I was gone. Never again, I determined; the sheriff could do it next time. Poor sheriff.

When you own your own company, you have to do some things you don't' want to do. To turn a paper down is to risk losing a client, and sending the paper out to the sheriff is simply losing hard cash. At the time, we had a girl serving papers for us on a part-time basis, but it would not be right to ask her to do our dirty work. Since I'd gotten away with serving the place the week before, I figured I could do it again. Besides, the corporation was being served, which meant one trip only – either I found the owner there, Rod Simon, or I would sub the paper on any employee I could find. Twenty bucks is twenty bucks; no complaint. I'd handle it.

14 – XYZ Towing, Again?

XYZ Towing is located in an industrial section of San Rafael, near the Bret Harte area. Big yellow tow trucks marked the spot. I parked the Tercel, took off my glasses and my watch, just in case, stuffed the paper into my pocket, and walked to the door.

Turning the knob of the door and finding it open, I smiled that smile I always smile when I know I've "got 'em." The feeling is one of the truly good feelings left in the world for me, one that doesn't result in cancer, weight gain or guilt.

Carefully, I stepped inside the tiny, dingy office— not as tiny and dingy as Terry and my lovely headquarters, but still tiny and dingy, and I found the place empty. A two-way radio set was on and squawking, two lights were lit up on a panel phone, but no humans. I began to feel a little creepy. Would I be remembered? Where was everybody?

Taking a deep breath, I called out, "Anybody home?"

In answer, Rod Simon himself opened the door of an adjoining office and said, "I'm home."

"Hello, Mr. Simon. I have a legal paper for XYZ Towing. Probably you're the person to give it to since you're the president. Right?"

Simon was not fearsome to behold. Ten years older, fifty pounds lighter and four inches shorter than me. I had many physical advantages over him. Yet, I didn't want to act discourteously as I knew others, no doubt, lurked about.

He hadn't come all the way into the room where I was, and I was fearful he would close the door and hide in his office. In that case, I would have left the paper anyway, but it would not have been the clean type of serve our company is famous for.

Happily, he didn't evade at all. Instead, he walked up to me, grabbed the paper from my hand, walked to the front door of the office, opened it, turned to me and yelled, "Out!"

Out was fine with me and I was. One step out the door, though, I heard another word, the word attack.

"Attack!"

That word meant one thing to me. Dog. The Tercel was ten yards away. My hand was on the door handle in less than a second. I swung the door open, jumped gracefully and perfectly into the seat and reached to close the door. Before I could get it all the way shut, a dog crashed into the side of it. A pit bull, one of my favorite kinds of dog, ranking right up there with Dobermans and shepherds. All lovely dogs.

It was an extremely narrow escape. Technically, Simon had committed assault, and I might have been able to have him arrested. However, no damage had been done to me or the car. A cop might have been hard put to go along with me on a citizen's arrest, and the district attorney's office probably wouldn't file on it. I decided to forget it and let the twenty dollars console me. But, never again.

Never again comes around far too often in the process serving business. Two weeks later, Terry was saying, "Here's another damn paper for XYZ Towing."

Terry knew, of course, about my previous problems with XYZ Towing, and he expected me to decline, as I did, but he didn't expect me to change my mind. Over a cup of coffee, I thought the thing out. How could I let myself be intimidated? If I refused this, where might it stop? Am I or am I not a process server? Couldn't I outsmart Simon and his dumb dog? Really, am I not a tough macho dude?

"Terry, I'm going to serve it," I announced some minutes later.

He only looked at me like I was crazy.

"I wouldn't do it."

"Well maybe you wouldn't, but I'm going to. Make out the work sheet for me, and I'll try it over the weekend."

"It's not going to be that easy, Kent. For the defendant, it reads, 'Rod Simon individually and doing business as XYZ Towing.' You've got to get him the first time or anybody the second, but it means two trips if you're not lucky the first time."

I'd decided, though, and I was going to stick. "Over the weekend, I'll get diligence on it, since it's a business that's open twenty-four hours a day, seven days a week. Then Monday, when Simon or a secretary is sure to be there, I'll drop it on one of them."

Saturday, I went by; Sunday, I went by. The door was locked but the place was operating, as I could tell calls were coming in.

Monday morning, as I drove to the office, I started thinking about Simon and the pit bull. It was possible to ask the San Rafael Police Department for an officer to accompany me; they will do it, but then I thought I'd get Terry out on it. Why not? I thought, no problem.

After Terry had settled into his morning, I said, "Terry, I'm doing XYZ today and I need you to back me up."

"I'm not going to do it."

"Why not? You know I'd do it for you."

"Maybe you don't like living as much as I do. Look, Kent, you didn't' have to take it but you did. We can still send it to the sheriff. But to hell with that dog crap."

Surely he had a good point. Yet, I couldn't turn it loose. And it wasn't the money. It was Simon and that dog; they weren't going to beat me. No question but that I'm still neurotic after all these years.

"Okay, Terry, you're right, forget about backing me up, but I'm going to do it."

"It's up to you. If I were you, I wouldn't. Those dogs go for your groin or your throat."

"Right."

"Groin or throat," a pleasant prospect for me as I drove over to XYZ. I planned to park my car better and strap on my big buck knife and let it stick out like a sore thumb. Not a bright move, but I was thinking groin or throat.

As soon as I turned into the parking area, I saw Simon seated in one of his two trucks working on something inside the cab. Things were looking good. I parked right behind the truck, stepped out quickly, leaving the engine running and the car door open. With paper in hand, I advanced on my target.

"Good morning, Mr. Simon. I have a legal paper for you individually and doing business as XYZ Towing."

He cocked his head around to see who was talking to him. "You must love it, or you wouldn't do it."

"Probably you are correct, Mr. Simon. Here's your paper."

Taking it from my hand like he did surprised me. No battle at all. Guess he figured I had him so why contest it. At any rate, I'd done it, and I smiled my smile.

Before retreating to my car, in no real hurry, I looked inside the cab of the truck. Lying on the seat, curled up and asleep was the pit bull. Not a twitch wrinkled his pub grey and black face. Sound asleep. Just how I like it. Good dog.

Chapter 15

Wild West Marin

West Marin is many things to many people. For some, it is a beautiful area to drive through on their way to the beach or to Mt. Tam. Others like it because it is different, away from the mainstream, definitely not suburban. Some years back, land and houses were cheaper "over-the-hill," and many Marinites saw their chance to own their own country place. Grass growers love the many hidden valleys, and dope dealers feel safe in the nearly inaccessible spots that aren't on anybody's map. And West Marin is a haven for dead beats.

In the last year and a half, I've ranged widely over rural Marin, roaming through every little town and village. Marin is predominantly little towns. I counted forty-two one time, with San Rafael the largest at around fifty-five thousand to Jewell on Sir Frances Drake Blvd. (not really a town, more of a entity declared by local citizens) where around twenty people are said to live.

There are a number of ways to approach West Marin. From the south, you can take Shoreline Highway off 101 through Mill Valley and Tam Junction and then either head for Muir Beach or climb halfway up Tamalpais and drop down into Stinson Beach. During the summer, I always wear a swimsuit in place of underwear, as I never know when I might need to serve a paper in Stinson. Southern California boy as I am, Stinson is as fine a beach as Zuma, Santa Monica, or Venice. If, per chance, I'm out by the beach and am caught without my swimsuit, I can head for Muir Beach, go through the rocks on the right side of the rather compact beachfront to the nudie beach where the tan-all-over Muir Beach club meets. Or, and this spot is even better, if I'm nearer Bolinas, I like Hagmeir Pond.

The longest route to West Marin is to go over Mt. Tam through Bolinas Road in Fairfax. Longest, but maybe the most spectacular, it is certainly the twistiest. Before you hit the mountain itself, in the foothills I suppose, you bypass Bon Tempe and Lagunitas Lakes, where there are plenty of trout. One of my fondest memories is of a very warm September day when my lady and I spread a blanket out along the remote shore of Bon Tempe and spent the afternoon skinny-dipping in the shimmering lake illegally and immorally, all adding up to joyfully. Yes, a bottle of Napa Valley wine, a roast beef sandwich from Perry's in Fairfax, along with a peaceful nap climaxing in a well-spent day in wonderland. Why do we do those things only once?

Leaving the lakes, heading still west, you reach the especially lovely Alpine Lake where you can even drive over a small dam. Large schools of giant bright orange-gold fish can often be seen cruising through the clear, deep water. Redwoods stand everywhere now, trails branching off, deer running, and hardly a soul around.

Climbing through the twists and turns of the backside of the mountain, the road severely narrows into what feels like a huge rain forest. Heavy mists are not uncommon in the area even on the hottest of days, and giant ferns and other evergreens threaten to choke the road closed.

Occasionally, there are breaks in the forest revealing vast expanses of meadow, gorgeous, free and untouched. Most impressive of all are the treeless hills that fall away to the cliffs overlooking the Pacific Ocean, especially when the sea breezes move their grasses in rhythmic waves of bronze and yellow.

When you go by way of the mountain lakes, you run into Highway 1 between Stinson Beach and Bolinas, nearer to Bolinas.

There is one other way, and that is via Sir Frances Drake Blvd. all the way to Highway 1. Drake begins at Highway 101 at Greenbrae, runs through Kentfield, Ross, San Anselmo, and Fairfax before it turns up hill, over White's Hill, then down into the valley on the other side. All of the other side is West Marin. Then, it's Woodacre, San Geronimo, Forest Knolls, Lagunitas, and beautiful Samuel P. Taylor State Park. Right at Drake and Highway 1 is the town of Olema, consisting of a couple of fine restaurants, a market, and a few houses. It's left then to Bolinas and Stinson Beach. Turning right leads you north, first to Point Reyes Station, wherein resides the Pulitzer Prize winning newspaper, The Point Reys Light. Then Marshall, where the notorious Synanon used to be, and further along is the upper Marin Coast. Jenner is up there somewhere as is Johnson's Oyster Farm. Before you reach the town of Point Reyes Station, there are turn-offs to Inverness and various beaches, including a very special one, Limantour. West Marin is honeycombed with exotic places, beaches, bays, villages, lodges, retreat centers and headquarters of various eastern religious groups. Marin and San Francisco are similar in that every turn seems to uncover an exciting discovery.

Process serving, then, is little more than sightseeing, leisurely cruises, fascinating places, and just plain fun. A serve that combined all of this and more was one involving a small claims paper for a gentleman residing in Forest Knolls.

The client was a guy Terry had run into while on his court run. Terry visits the civic center at least once every weekday. The window for filing civil papers is right next to the window where people file small claims suits. My partner has been given small claims papers to serve by the plaintiffs filing them while standing in line at the civil window. There are many off-beat, even crazy claims that people file, and not many people know what they are really doing. We've run into some rather bizarre situations when taking private small claims cases.

Charles Robison hadn't paid for a set of tires he'd bought for his four-wheel drive Bronco. The San Rafael businessman who had sold Robison the tires wanted his money. After numerous requests by letter and phone, our plaintiff had decided to sue. There was a chance it would work, if the paper could be served, but there are no guarantees even when service is completed. A lot of people simply do not care.

Charles Robison had no address. I had only the street he lived on. Of course, he wasn't listed in the phone book. The tire salesman suggested asking around at homes on the road. On first consideration, I didn't think that would be a problem, but the day I got down to actually doing it, I wished I hadn't gotten myself so committed.

It takes a while to get out to Forest Knolls, about twenty-five minutes from my house. I wasn't looking forward to hunting for Robison, but I wanted to give it a try. The plaintiff had prepaid, and I thought it would be nice to deposit the check rather than mail it back. So a-knocking I went.

Everyone I turned up knew Robison, and everyone knew where he lived. However, I couldn't' get any precise directions. It was always, "Robison, oh yeah, he lives just up a little. Look for his green truck." After a half-hour, I got a pretty good fix on Robison's place. But no one would come out and plainly tell me. The people I talked to were mostly in their thirties, hippy looking still, or maybe redneck is more accurate, home grown country folk, dressed countryish, not stylishly, lots of hair, and it seemed they became somewhat paranoid when they heard Robison's name. I was beginning to become a little wary about the nature and/or habits of Mr. Charles Robison.

The way to Robison's house was complex. It was necessary to enter the driveway of a completely different person, wind around that house, drive right across the backyard to reach a tiny wooden bridge under which a small stream ran during the rainy season, carry on through a field with a cluster of chicken houses set at the far end. Midway across the field, I began looking for the green truck amidst the dozen or so shacks and coops. No truck was in sight. I did find a dog, however, that ran up to the car and was nearly able to look me in the eye.

Pulling up in front of a chicken coop, one of the long ones, Petaluma style, I studied the barking dog. The tail was wagging. I didn't want to leave without attempting to find Robison, so I hoped the friendly sign was reliable. The dog, some kind of mongrel, quieted down and only followed me around as I searched for the defendant. At that point, I figured I was wasting my time.

There wasn't any house-type house. There was one tiny wooden and tarpaper shack that looked like a poor choice to live in. The grass was high, in some places waist high, and there was debris everywhere.

To be safe, I decided to call out Robison's name.

"Charles, Charles, anybody here?"

Silence was the only response. The dog's heavy

breathing was audible along with the wind rustling the tall grass.

It was a lovely setting. Green and yellow pasture, broken down fences, horses grazing nearby, picturesque barns standing vacant, pines on the hills, and a warm sun cheering up the afternoon. Convinced now that no one was around, I sat down in a metal folding chair that was set up next to a shack and enjoyed the sights and the smells.

After ten or so minutes, I got up to leave and began walking back to the car. Rounding the corner of a dilapidated barn, I ran right into two people laid out naked on two aluminum lounges. The man, whom I guessed was Robison, had a great big shotgun lying on his chest. The lady didn't have room for anything else on her chest. She was the first genuine redhead I'd ever seen.

"Excuse me, I didn't' know you were here. Are you Mr. Robison?"

"You've got five seconds to leave."

There was absolutely no point in pursuing the matter. Abruptly, I turned and walked stiffly and rapidly to the car. I wasn't afraid; I was mad at Robison.

As I passed the shack that looked like the living quarters, I slid the small claims paper under the door. No way was I going to pay Robison another visit.

I got in the car, turned the ignition on, backed around, was ready to leave, then shouted out, "Robison – I served you a small claims paper. It's in your shack. You are served."

We deposited that check.

Chapter 16

A Change of Pants

Collection attorneys make the best clients for a process server, since they have a high volume of lawsuits. Their slogan is often, "Sue the bastards." My two favorite such legal firms are "Sue'em and Screw'em," and "Milk'em and Bilk'em."

That all sounds rather negative; I mean it only for fun. The attorneys for collection agencies have a low reputation with other attorneys, but I've found them to be a decent lot. There is no question but that their work is critical for many businesses and individuals who are depending on the collection of bad debts for their survival. No, I don't have any problems with collection attorneys. The lawyers I don't appreciate are those who defend people whom they know are guilty and willingly lie and conceal the truth so some unhinged rogue can get off, and divorce attorneys who create a hostile environment between a husband and wife to ensure the suit will proceed rather than be mended through reconciliation. Law is very often a dirty business.

Shortly after Terry and I began our partnership, we created a brochure to aid in selling our services. Collection attorneys were my number one target. As I went from law office to law office, I kept hearing the name Abbott Everett in response to my question, "Do you know any collection attorneys?"

Everett's office is on Fifth Avenue in San Rafael, in one of the Victorian houses converted into offices. Only Everett's name appeared on the "shingle" by the front door. It was a cold call; I didn't phone ahead. Coming up the stairs, I could see, through the bay window, the secretary seated at her desk. Opening the door without knocking, I stepped up to the desk.

"Good morning. I'm Kent Philpott. My partner, Terry Cuddy and I are process servers, and we'd like to work for you. Is Mr. Everett in?"

"Oh gee," the secretary said, "We already have one."

"We're better, at least I'd like to show you what we can do."

"Maybe you'd better talk to Mr. Everett."

Sometimes a lawyer handles all the office business, sometimes a great deal is left to the legal secretary. If the secretary took care of who did the process serving, I would not want to jump over her head. In this case, Everett himself was the decision maker.

Abbott Everett gave me what I interpreted to be a hostile look. Maybe he thought I was a debtor come to do him in. His face didn't change much as I announced who I was.

"Process server? Well, I have one."

"Are you sure you couldn't give us a try sometime? At least, let me leave a brochure. Our specialty is we never charge you unless we make the serve. No proof of service, no bill."

My little spiel took all of twenty seconds. Everett's face softened. I was getting somewhere.

"Maybe I'll try you out. Lately I've been dissatisfied with the people handling my stuff. We'll see."

16 – A Change of Pants

And with that, he went back into his office and closed the door.

When I returned to my office, I told Terry about Everett. He said, "We'll see." I thought my efforts deserved a "Hey, good work," not a "We'll see."

Some days later, a letter came from Abbott Everett with an OEX, that is, an Order of Examination and Order to Appear, for a John Frank with two addresses: The Olympic Club on Post Street in San Francisco and a business address of 482 Market Street, fifteenth floor, number 1504. The accompanying cover letter explained that it was an old case. Some two years earlier, Frank had let an unlawful detainer suit go to default and had never paid the judgment. Every previous attempt to serve him had met with failure.

Everett was indeed putting us to the test. We were going to have to earn his business the hardest possible way—serving an OEX on a real evader. I got on it the very next day. My first stop was the Olympic Club. I'd read about the famous place in Herb Cain's column a few times, but I didn't have a clue as to what the club was all about. No doubt, I reasoned, it was a hide-out for some of San Francisco's elite gentlemen.

The Olympic Club impressed me. There was a doorman, a reception desk, other servants of sorts walking about, and the huge entrance hall was exquisitely furnished. The uniformed man at the front desk did know of Frank and made some inquiries to see if Frank was there. After some minutes, I was informed that Frank had left the club for the day. Though I had struck out on my initial attempt, I was at least learning something about John Frank.

Parking is terrible around 482 Market. The only hope is to look south of the street for a space. Around and around

I went, growing more and more irritated. A parking ticket can be incredibly costly, and the meter maids are the grossest bunch of vultures under the sun. The first decent place I found allowed for a mere fifteen minutes. A quarter for fifteen minutes; that's a dollar an hour. A minute late and I would earn a twenty-buck ticket, or perhaps the car would be towed. It is a nearly desperate situation. Such conditions must be doing genuine harm to retail business in the area.

Fifteen minutes wouldn't do, so, around and around again, turning left off Market illegally every once in a while, hoping and praying, eyes on the rear-view mirror, looking for a city oasis, a place to park. After twenty full minutes, I snagged a space on Third Street below Mission. And I could stay there a whole hour! A dream come true. I was going to get John Frank one way or the other.

Walking down Market, I came across an urban McDonald's, this one on the odd numbered or south side of Market, in the five hundred block. I stopped in for a cone; I'm addicted, but now they don't seem much like ice cream. Still, I haven't been able to break the habit. Must be the sugar that's got me.

Down the street I strode, with the vanilla-tasting white thing in a cone in my hand, the OEX in my pocket, a cruel smile on my face, twenty-five bucks to be made circling in my thoughts, hot-footing it to 482 Market.

John Frank was supposed to be on the fifteenth floor of your typical old office building, the kind with the huge marble urinals in the bathrooms that lend an air of sophistication to that most basic function. This men's room even had wainscoting of what was probably mahogany. That era is definitely over. Anyway, I found the elevator, which lurched me up to the proper floor.

The hallway I stepped into ran thirty or so yards. There

were no side corridors; each end held a staircase. The elevator was in the center, and eight doors were evenly spaced along the walls. The ceiling must have been eleven feet up there, solid dark wood paneling ran up to eight feet with glass the last three feet. There were no numbers on the doors, nor titles, nor anything, and a quick check revealed only four of the offices were occupied. This was cleverly accomplished by observing which offices had lights on in them.

As quietly as possible, I tested the doorknobs of the offices with the lights on in them. Only two would turn. A woman about forty was seated behind a desk in the first one I tried. It was nearly bare of furniture or decoration. There was one desk, one chair, one woman, one phone, one old picture of George Washington on the wall, and that was it.

The woman was as odd as the room.

"Hi, I'm trying to find John Frank."

A pair of brown eyes riveted on me. "John Frank. Yes, I believe he is on this floor, but I don't know which office."

"There is a John Frank Senior and a John Frank Junior; do you know which is here?"

This was a lie on my part—a ploy, not really a lie.

"Oh, I think he is an older man, in his seventies. But I don't know. I've never seen him."

Running her answer across my mind, I wondered how she could guess at his age without having seen him, but I thought it best not to press it. I also wondered what she was up to.

"I see you're quite busy," another ploy, "What is your business?"

"Oh, this isn't a business. I just come here and talk to my friends on the phone. I can't stand being at home, you know, my mother is crazy, so I stay here all day."

There were no windows, a cubbyhole if ever there was one, and I noticed several men's magazines, adult stuff, on her desk. She had a funny look on her face and her hands weren't any longer on top of the desk. I'd go on but I don't want it to seem like I'm too terribly sexually oriented. Turning back to the hallway, I supposed that the sins of the mother had been visited upon the daughter. However, it could have been the other way around.

Now, my anticipation grew as I walked to the other open door. Before entering, I listened for a moment, trying for a clue of any kind. But nothing.

Again, I found a tiny windowless room with a desk and little else in it. Seated behind the desk was an old man reading the Wall Street Journal. He had it spread open flat on the top of the desk, and leaning over it, he reminded me of a hungry buzzard.

"Mr. Frank?" I asked expectantly. The heart was pounding. My fingers closed around the legal paper in my pocket. "How are you, Mr. Frank?"

The old gentleman raised his head to look at me. Without changing expression, his eyes caught me for a moment then dropped again to the newspaper.

"Well, Mr. Frank – I have a legal paper for you." I took it out of my pocket and laid it on his desk. He saw that move, stood up, folded the newspaper, held it up to my face and asked, "Whose name is that on the label?"

"Julian Crocker," I read.

"That's who I am. Get out!"

He sat back down, unfolded his newspaper, laid it out on the desk and went back to his reading. I had been dismissed. There was nothing to do but pick up the OEX and leave. He had me. Walking to the elevator, I felt confused and embarrassed. If I'd left the paper and been wrong, it could be serious. Failure to appear is contempt of court, a

16 – A Change of Pants

criminal charge. And the potential for disaster was considerable. Without question, I was going to have to call Abbot Everett for a description of Frank. Unhappily, I was in the process of failing in my attempt to impress a new client.

The following morning, I called Everett to see if I could get the description. Everett told me he hadn't handled the initial suit and so had never seen Frank. He did suggest my talking to the plaintiff directly for the help I needed. Seemingly Everett did not object to my call and knew that serving Frank was going to be tough. He did not act surprised at my difficulty and actually sympathized with me. It may have been that most of the process servers in Marin and San Francisco had tried already. If I got Frank, when I got Frank, the company would look real good, and we stood a good chance of picking up a potentially profitable client.

Soon as I hung up from talking to Everett, I called the plaintiff, a Susan Peabody, an old woman who was only too happy to describe John Frank for me. She'd been after him forever and had nearly given up hope. For the first time, I found out Frank was a lawyer, forty years old, blond, blue eyes, six feet tall, medium build and good looking. And, of course, he was a sailor with his own yacht, which was berthed in Sausalito. Mrs. Peabody wished me good luck and I told her I would try very hard.

Most of our work is in Marin and I don't like to go into the City unless I have three or more papers. As it happened, I didn't have enough serves to justify another trip that very week, so a week passed before I made another attempt.

It was a Thursday when I went back in, and Thursdays are good for work in the City; it is too early to take off on a three-day weekend. Wednesday night is not usually a party night, meaning people may be expected to show up

Thursday. But I've found it's not wise to be earlier than nine or later than eleven thirty. The two- and one-half hours between eleven-thirty and two are dead serving-wise. Whenever I did a stakeout on a businessperson or a secretary, eleven-thirty is generally the hour I take up my vigil. Everyone goes to lunch.

Eleven-thirty sharp, I was at my post at 482 Market Street. The exact same offices had lights on. Two doors were unlocked; two were locked. The old man was in place again as was the woman with the funny look on her face. Two offices, right next to each other were locked. Using my superior strength, I pulled myself up to the window by grasping the two-inch ledge between solid wall and glass top. Both offices were empty, but the open door between them showed they were connected. It was indeed a lawyer's office. There were papers on a desk, and I could see steam rising from a coffee cup on the desk. But there was not a soul to be seen. Since there was no way out but the hall I was in, I was a bit mystified. Someone had to be there. The only hiding place would have been under the desk. Either that or there was a secret passage hidden somewhere in the wall-to-wall bookcases.

There was no option but to wait. The lights were on. A cup of coffee, hot enough to give off steam, set on the desk. I had to wait. My plan was to sit on the floor between the door and the elevator just across from the stair well. There would be no escape. To make my wait more tolerable, I jogged across and up Market to McDonald's for a light snack. To make sure Frank would not get by me, I got off at the second floor, hit the elevator's stand-by button, took to the stairs and managed to get back to the second floor before anyone had used the elevator.

I'd finished off my Big Mac, a milk and a small order of fries before one of the doors in question opened and my man stepped into the hall. One look told me it was John Frank. The description was perfect; I had him, and I thrilled inside, almost shuddering. Scrambling to my feet as quickly as I could, I said, "Hello, Mr. Frank. As you can see I've been waiting for you."

Frank said nothing; he even tried to not look at me. No question but that he was extremely startled. As fast as he could, he walked to the elevator and hit the button.

Moving up alongside him, I stood and looked at him. Right color hair, right height and weight, right age, handsome, casual clothes and top-siders, the new kind made of leather. It was definitely John Frank.

Politely but firmly I held out the paper. "I've got an Order of Examination for you."

Turning furiously to me he nearly shouted, "I'm not Frank."

"You are not John Frank?"

"No, I'm not."

"You look like him, just like him. So much so that I think you are."

"The hell I am."

"Then who are you?"

"My name isn't Frank."

"Can you prove it, like with a license?"

He slapped his left rear pants packet saying, "I don't have my wallet with me."

He was looking desperate.

"Well, I think you are John Frank. Here's your paper."

The elevator arrived at that point. He stepped in as I let the paper flutter to the floor. I did it with a smile. The elevator door slid closed, and he was gone.

Since there was only one elevator, I punched the button in and began filling out my work sheet. It was a good serve even though the document was lying at my feet and

Frank was gone.

The elevator door opened and, much to my surprise, John Frank was standing there. It wasn't that he had a mean look on his fact. I'd say it was an expression of utter embarrassment. As he walked past me, I noticed he was holding the pants on his left leg away from his body. I watched him retreat down the hall to his office and couldn't resist calling after him, "You are served John Frank."

I stood there long enough to see him go into his office and slam the door. Fortunately, I glanced down at the elevator floor as I got in. There, in the middle, was a puddle of slightly yellow liquid. The smell told me it was pee. Now I knew why Frank was holding his pants away from his leg and why he went back to his office. Frank had peed his pants.

Rather than being highly elated and amused by the encounter, I felt somewhat saddened. Yes, I was glad to have done my job and maybe won a new client, but I had mixed emotions about John Frank. I had no way of knowing all that was behind the case. Obviously, it had substantial meaning for Frank and for Susan Peabody. My role, I realized, was little more than a tiny part in a long story, a rude interruption in what was probably a complex human drama. There is always a story, and there are always feelings, always money, sometimes crisis, and sometimes tragedy. I was there not to help, counsel, or befriend. I wasn't there to damage or condemn. I was there, just for a moment, a messenger of bad news. But for Mrs. Peabody, I was going to be an angel. For Everett, I was going to be a good process server. For John Frank, among other things, I was a change of pants.

Chapter 17

When Process Serving Becomes Ministerial

Cypress in Fairfax is off Laurel, which is off Cascade, which is off Bolinas. I needed 320 Cypress. Going off Laurel is the back way, but it puts you closer to the three hundred block area than if you took Cypress off Bolinas.

By this time, I've become very familiar with Cypress Street, having been there serving papers a half dozen times or so. My first time up Cypress, I had domestic papers: an order for a hearing concerning visitation rights which I had to serve on a mother and her daughter. A child must be served in the presence of an adult. In this case, it meant serving mother and daughter at the same time. It didn't figure to be easy, since the ex-husband wanted to take the girl away from her mother.

The driveway up to the house was steep, and the stairs leading to the front door were steep as well. Walking up the stairs, I could feel the warm house; someone was home. The open front door looked good to me. I knocked on the outside doorframe. Again, I knocked, and a third time. No response. Calling out, I banged on a window. Still, there was nothing. A big grey cat brushed by my feet as I waited.

Finally, I turned away and climbed down the stairs – a waste of time and considerable energy, I thought to myself as I got back behind the wheel of the Tercel.

That first attempt was in the early morning, a Saturday, and as I drove back in from West Marin about noon, I stopped at Fairfax's Cala Market on Sir Frances Drake to call the woman and see what might happen if I told her what the situation was. There was not much to lose by tipping her off. It seemed probable that she knew the papers were coming. At least that would explain the warm house and no one answering my knock.

Fortunately, the mother's name was in the phone book. There was no street listed, just the phone number. Loretta, the mother, answered the ring and I explained who I was and what I had. She began crying on the phone, crying that conveyed to me a great sadness. I let her make up her mind, telling her I wouldn't serve her or make any further attempts unless she agreed to it. She regained her composure and asked me to drive up with the papers. Leaving the pay phone in front of Cala Market, I felt smug and satisfied with the success of my tactic.

The fog had burned off around ten, and the day was already into the mid-eighties. Loretta was sitting in a chair by the open front door, crying as I tapped lightly on the doorframe. Looking up at me, she waved me in.

Before me was one of the most beautiful women I'd ever seen— tan and blonde with a model's face, about thirty-five years old, with white short shorts, my favorite thing. More than her beauty, I saw her grief and despair. A man who had left her before her child was even born now wanted the little girl, age seven, and Loretta knew it would be a long, tragic, and costly affair, even if she won what would certainly be a dirty court battle.

Sitting down near her, I put off my process serving hat

and donned my ministerial garments. For some minutes, she couldn't speak to me. Though I'm no expert, I thought it possible she might be in the process of a breakdown. Slowly I pointed out several advantages of a hearing before a judge. It would be a way of settling issues and having uncertainties defined. She would have a chance to tell her story and have a judgment imposed that would legally prevent her ex from taking her little girl.

After what seemed to me to be forever, Loretta began wiping her eyes and clearing her throat. For the next thirty or so minutes, she told me her story, and she told me of her little girl, Karen. Even though I was hearing only one side of a two-sided story, it appeared that if it were only partially true, she and Karen had been seriously aggrieved. The papers were yet in my pocket.

For an hour or more we talked. It was very much like a counseling session. Loretta had been through much grief in her adult life, yet her resiliency and courage amazed me. And she was a talented actress, a model, an animationist, and a lovely, mature woman.

I did pull the papers out finally.

"Loretta, you know I have these papers for you and Karen. But I won't give them to you unless you want me to." Odd thing is I really meant it.

"It's okay. I'll take them."

"Well, one is for you, but as strange as it may seem, I have to give Karen her copy personally."

"Oh, I know. I was a legal secretary. I'll get her."

Loretta disappeared into a bedroom at the end of a hall. In a few minutes she was back with the little girl. Karen had brown curly hair, a sweet shy face, and she sat down by her mommy on the sofa.

"Karen, I have a paper, a letter, to give you. Your mom knows what it is and will tell you about it."

I held it out for her and a little hand received it. She placed it on her lap and folded her hands on top of it. Her brown eyes looked up at me as I smiled down at her.

"You are real cute, Karen. You're your mommy's special girl. I think both you and your mom are wonderful."

Even as I spoke them, the words felt dumb to me. It seemed I had to reach so far to express what I was feeling and missed the mark. The smile and the tiny hug I gave Karen was no doubt better understood than anything I could think to say.

That was in August. Loretta would occasionally call me, and I stopped in on them a few times. I knew if I let myself, and Loretta would have let me, I could have entered right into their lives. But it seemed that was not my role. I was to be a minister to them.

All contact with Loretta and Karen ceased about the first week in January. I saw them at Christmas when I dropped by some presents for them. Somewhere around the middle of April, I opened a letter from a client and once again saw Loretta's name. The client was her landlord, and the envelope contained a summons and complaint for unlawful detainer. Reading the complaint, it didn't look good. She was several months down in rent. I hated to see it. I didn't want to serve it; yet, I figured it was better me than an absolute stranger.

When I called, Loretta was happy to see me, and she wasn't shocked to find out why I was there. A movie she'd counted on hadn't come through and the job mix-up had left her in serious financial trouble. She'd tried to work things out with the landlord, but he wasn't going to give in.

What little I could do, I did: stalling, saying I couldn't serve the paper because no one was home, which necessitated a posting, all aimed at buying time for Loretta and Karen. Loretta especially wanted Karen to finish out the school year. That would take some doing.

Loretta's legal training paid off. She filed an answer all on her own, arguing motions, forcing a jury trial, which she lost, of course, but it all bought time. And we talked often, on the phone and at her place. Still, I was the minister. Through the legal and emotional struggle, I watched a brave woman face a harsh reality. Often it looked to me like a fight for survival with the outcome unclear. Sometimes I could see she was hanging on by a thread.

In May, Loretta landed a full-time job. The court battle on the unlawful detainer was going on, and her delaying tactics were working. Karen was going to finish the school year at her Fairfax school.

The first week in June, I got a call from Loretta. She was crying, crying hard. Her words were getting mixed up, so I told her I'd be right over. Terry, my partner, asked me what was up when he saw me heading for the door.

"Terry, it's Loretta. I've got to go. She sounds bad."

"Call me as soon as you can and get back as soon as you can."

Loretta was propped up on her white wicker couch when I walked in.

"Kent, thank you for coming. I felt I really needed to talk to you."

Grabbing a kitchen chair, I set it up near the couch. "Loretta, are you sick?"

"Yes, I've got some kind of stomach flu. I haven't been able to hold anything down for two days."

She didn't look good to me. Her usual bright face was shallow and pale. There was no sparkle in her pretty blue eyes.

"Kent, look at this though."

A pile of papers that had been lying on her lap was now lifted to me. On top was an eviction notice from the sheriff.

Loretta had been denied a jury trial, and a muni judge had allowed the judgment to be entered against her. The lockout was scheduled for noon the very next day.

That was serious, since Cypress had been reduced to a "not a through street" due to one of the many slides from the big 1982 storm. And even though an access road had been constructed linking Cypress up with Oak Street, no vehicle larger than a light pickup was allowed in. Thus, there was no way to move Loretta out.

The second paper in the pile was a notice of garnishment of wages. Loretta said her employer was really pleased about it, about as much as she was. And, naturally enough, Loretta felt her new boss would now be prejudiced against her.

Then there was a notice that her bank account had been attached. All her money, what little she had been able to make was gone.

And the fourth paper was a small claims paper she'd been served from her landlord concerning a long-disputed PG&E bill.

Nor was that all. Her boyfriend was in the hospital having undergone surgery that very morning.

There she lay, clear-eyed now, talking about what she planned to do. Karen would be able to finish up the last couple of school weeks by staying at a friend's house. The small claims suit she'd pay off a little at a time. She'd get the judgment paid off in ten mouths at the present rate of garnishment, and she'd move. The money from her account—what was gone was gone.

I listened, nodded, and wondered. This was some woman. What a lucky boyfriend. The odds were long against her, and it might take considerable time, but I felt confident for Loretta.

Chapter 18

Very Professional

Jean lived on Elm Street above San Francisco Theological Seminary. Driving through the school, I reminisced about the years I had spent studying at the seminary for my doctorate. Before I had been a student there, I used the library to write two books. Whenever I see that library—strong and beautiful, clean and white—it reminds me of Louise Beck, who for many years was the faithful and most gracious librarian. How far away I felt from my student years in the theological seminary, as I made my way to serve a legal paper.

Jean's house was set at least one hundred yards off the road, straight up. I groaned with dismay the first wintery evening my flashlight revealed the dozens of wooden steps set into the hillside. Up, up and away they went to a big rambling three-story wood house surrounded by oaks and madrones. The house had long been neglected, fences were broken down, and the yards around the place were a tangle. Piles of boards lay everywhere, as did used electrical equipment and carpentry tools. It seemed to me that a workingman lived there, a person who was so busy working on other people's projects he didn't have the time and energy to take care of his own doings. And, on top of it all, he owed someone money.

Not the first, not the second, not the third, but the fourth attempt was the one that did it. When I finally found Jean Robeard, I remarked to him about the sound physical shape he must be in having to climb the steep stairs so often. Jean looked at me briefly as I made my statement and abruptly closed the door on me. French descent evidently, he had a rugged handsome look closely akin to that of Robert Redford.

Roughly a year after the initial serving of the summons and complaint on Robeard, an OEX came in for him. I did not remember him or the steps as I made out the work sheet, but as soon as I turned onto Elm, the climb up the hill flashed nastily in my mind. The thought of chugging up the stairs was too much for me, so I tucked the paper back into my briefcase. Another day.

An OEX is a dated document, thereby making it difficult to forget it too long. At that time, an OEX had to be served three days before the hearing date. That three-day requirement has now become ten. And an OEX cannot be sub-served; it must be delivered personally. With a few weeks remaining before the court date, I did make it up the hillside. It was in the evening with just enough light to find my way without the aid of a flashlight. With no light at all, the steps would have been dangerous.

The house, as I've already mentioned, is large. My knock at the front door brought no response. But lights burned, and I could hear people talking. Carefully I walked around to the back door, always alert for dogs. Standing before the door, I could plainly hear voices. That thrill of excitement went through me, the high anticipation of getting my man.

I knocked firmly on the glass portion of the door. In a

second, a teenage girl opened the door. To her left, standing at a sink doing dishes was the person whom I thought was Jean Robeard.

"Hi," I said to the girl, "is Jean here?"

"He's not here," the man at the sink answered.

The Jean Robeard I remembered had a beard; this man was clean-shaven.

"When will he be back?"

"In a week."

"Okay, I'm Jim Ross. You can tell him I stopped by."

Back down the long flight of stairs I went with a funny feeling. The excitement had turned to discouragement, and I just knew I'd been suckered. Problem was, I wasn't' sure, not completely, and with an OEX, I couldn't' take a chance. The idea of trying again didn't please me much.

I let it go until almost the last moment. The Saturday before the Monday court date, I drove down Elm once again. Pulling up to the address, I found the guy who had been washing dishes the time before, talking to another guy. They were standing beside an old green pickup truck. My blood pressure was rising, and the thrill was on me as I turned the ignition off and reached to the passenger seat for Jean Robeard's paper. Calming myself, I slowly opened the door, swung out and crossed the street to the truck and the men. As I approached, the one guy I'd never seen before began walking away. With great joy, I hear him call back, "See you Jean."

Ambling up to the truck, I gave my man a smile and a hello. Setting my left foot up on the truck's rear bumper and resting my elbows on the truck's sides, I asked, "Doing a little hauling today?"

"Yeah, carting some stuff up the hill."

"Remember me? Jim Ross. I was here a while back. I was asking for Jean Robeard."

"Sure, I remember."

"Well, here I am again. Is he around today?"

"No, he was back, but he's in Europe now."

"Europe, huh?"

"France actually; he's French. I have his address if you'd like to write. He's going to be gone quite a while."

I was tongue-in-cheek, but I felt Jean was still trying to fool me. "What is your name?"

"Uh, John, John Roberts."

"John Roberts?"

He nodded yes.

"I heard your friend call you Jean."

"Oh," he said with a bit of a smile, a tiny one really, but I saw it.

"You are Jean Robeard. Right?"

He was silent, eyes to the ground.

"Unless you can prove you aren't, Jean, I'm leaving this legal paper."

To that point, I hadn't taken the paper out of my pocket. Laying it on the bed of the truck, I smiled and stepped back waiting for a response.

"You know, I thought Jean had a beard."

"He did; he shaved it."

"That made it tricky for me."

"I must say you are very professional."

"Thank you. By the way, this is an Order of Examination, and it is scheduled for this Monday morning. It's best not to miss it. They tend to come out for you with a bench warrant."

"I'll mail this to Jean in France."

"That's a great idea."

That night, I was taking son Vernon and ex-wife, Bobbie, to see Spielberg's Poltergeist at the Tamalpais Theater on Drake in San Anselmo. It was the first weekend the film was in Marin and everybody and their brother was out to see it. Starting out two hours early, we were nearly first in line for the last showing of the evening. A long line stretched back to the Taco Bell. Standing in line waiting, I thought I saw a familiar face. I nudged Bobbie and Vernon.

"I think that's Jean, the guy I was telling you about."

"Where?" Vern asked.

"In the ticket line. The guy with the grey coat and bushy hair."

The man with the familiar face had to go past us after buying his tickets. He caught my eye, and I smiled. Walking up to me, he extended his right hand, which I took.

"Hi, Jean."

Without admitting a thing, he leaned slightly towards Bobbie. "He's very professional. Hope you enjoy the film."

Chapter 19

It Goes with the Territory

There is no doubt that process servers complain a lot. That includes me. On some days, I've gotten four out of five serves and on others, I've missed a dozen straight. One Saturday morning, my first nine attempts resulted in zip; then I got the next seven in a row. It's the back-to-back losing days that get you. By the time you have four or five in a row, the complaints are liable to roll off the tongue like butter.

Terry is the one I roll to. Dragging on his cigarette (he has since quit smoking) between sips of coffee, his blue eyes study me under the salt and pepper bushy eyebrows. His common response is, "It goes with the territory." He was the first person I heard who used that cliché.

"It goes with the territory," brings me little comfort; it is an explanation, a "why" to some of the things that happen. For instance, attorneys are not above sending us papers they know are unservable. However, they want us to check out certain addresses just to see. Our policy of "no service, no fee" means such clients get a lot of free information, valuable on the field skip tracing. But it goes with the territory.

19 – It Goes with the Territory

The following is a list of events, circumstances and realities that go with the territory.

Sitting in a car many long miles
Worn out tires and brakes
Frequent stops at gas stations
Dip stick shows low on oil
Front end of car out of alignment again
Messy car interior
Dirty car exterior
Doors slammed in the face
Barking dogs
Attacking dogs
Being cussed at
Being challenged to fights
Ordered off property
Being looked down the nose at
Trips to the courthouse
Dirt roads up the sides of hills
Crawling up narrow trails at night
Pounding heart waiting for doors to open
Complaints from attorneys
No appreciation for a job well done
The fear that a bullet may come through a door
Attorneys who don't pay their bills
Meeting people in desperate plights
Meeting women at home who insist you stay a while
Easy money

The last entry has some truth to it. Terry and I were talking things over one morning when a guy called wanting to hire an investigator. We get really excited when a call comes in for investigative work. P.I. work is more lucrative, and we enjoy saying we're investigators rather than process servers. But serving is still our bread and butter.

The caller wanted to know if there was a warrant out for his arrest. He explained he had nearly been caught in a drug bust some five months previously. The cops had been making the raid on his partners as he drove up. Rather than presenting himself to the police, he had made a quick trip to the San Jose airport and had taken off on a five-month vacation. His car was still parked in the airport's car lot. Five months had been long enough, he felt. He wanted to come back home, but he had to know where he stood. I could follow the conversation on the phone between Terry and the caller enough to catch the drift.

"I can do some checking. Take one week to do a thorough job."

Pause. Terry wrinkled his nose and puffed on his Parliament.

"Two fifty."

Pause. A smile lit up Terry's face. "Sure. Meet you in front of Shakey's in ten minutes."

Hanging up, Terry tilted his chair back and swung his boots up on the desk. "Looks like we hit a good one."

"Sounds like it. And I hear he's showing up next door. Was that 'two fifty' two hundred and fifty dollars?"

"Certainly was."

Ten minutes later, Terry walked over to Shakey's to meet our client, and in another ten minutes, he was back. His thick mustache couldn't hide the grin as he reached into his pocket and pulled out two one-hundred-dollar bills and one fifty. He stuffed one big bill in my shirt pocket, kept one himself and put the fifty in our deposit bag.

"A nice day's work."

"How do we handle this, Terry? We must have to do something."

"You can take off in two hours. Go over to the municipal court in Oakland and check the active and inactive criminal file at the clerk's office and see if our guy's name appears. You do that and I'll check my police connection and that will be that."

"So, if there is a warrant out for him, this is the way to find out?"

"That's it."

"Got it." Be back in a couple of hours."

The drive to Oakland consumed forty-five minutes, a dime to park, one flight of stairs, fifteen minutes at a counter thumbing through two big books and back to the car, the freeway, and the office. There was no indication that any action had been taken against our client. Terry had made his calls and could find no problem either.

"That's it, Terry?"

"That's it."

"Let's go to lunch."

"Yeah, let me get that fifty."

"Good idea."

That was good territory. Of course, there is the other. We had gotten a summons and complaint from a new client, a Donald Washburn. He wanted service as soon as possible on a corporation, and we were to serve the principal, an Andy Matucci. There was one address, one of the "Corte" streets in Greenbrae. Hoping to impress the new client with our swift and efficient serve, I hopped right on it that evening. The house was vacant, and there was not a clue as to where the previous occupant had gone, not even a realtor's "For sale" sign. I then turned to the phone book and looked up the company name. Much to my surprise, there it was in black and white. The corporation had an address in San Rafael, 1000 Fourth Street, Courthouse Square. It struck me that the lawyer should have given us the business address.

Next morning, I parked on A Street, opposite the drive-up window at the California Canadian Bank. Finding not even a penny in my pocket, I walked over to the newsstand next to the Rafael Theater to buy a pack of Orbit gum and thereby get some change. In the brief moment I was gone, I earned a seven-buck ticket. Oh well.

Up to the fourth floor by elevator, down the hall to Wells and Mines, Inc.; but all I found was a locked door. Down the hall, I walked into an office and asked the receptionist if she knew anything about Wells and Mines, Inc. She told me she knew next to nothing about them and what she did know was that the office was rarely open, and then only in the mornings.

One other tack to take was calling the old home phone number to see if there was a new number. There was – A Sausalito number, which I called immediately and found myself talking to the defendant, Andy Matucci.

"Mr. Matucci; this is Jim Ross. I was hoping for an appointment. In fact, I was by your San Rafael office earlier this morning."

"I've closed out the business. I use the office only for personal matters now."

"You're out of business?"

"Oh, yes."

"Mr. Matucci, I have to be honest with you. I have a legal paper for you, and I wonder if we could arrange a time I could drop it off to you."

"A legal paper? Whom is it from?"

"I'd like to tell you, but I've found I get in a lot of hot water when I do."

"Is it from George Schmidt?"

"Well, yes it is."

"Tell him I've got a check in the mail."

"Really?"

19 – It Goes with the Territory

"Right, that will take care of it."

"Okay Mr. Matucci. Thank you."

Immediately I called Donald Washburn and reported my conversation with Matucci. He wanted me to hold the paper for a few days but in the meantime, see if I could get the home address.

The phone number was all I could get from the operator; but the telephone company's business office gave me the address. It was up on Wolfback Ridge in Sausalito on Cloud Nine Road. Nothing short of a major expedition is sufficient to fight through the fog and other obstacles in that area to locate anybody.

A few days later, I called Washburn to see if Matucci had in fact mailed in a check. Of course, he hadn't. Washburn urged me to make the serve as quickly as I could. I promised I would work diligently on it.

And I did. Over a period of forty-four days, I made twenty-six attempts, Terra Linda to Sausalito, back and forth, many miles, fog, hills, dark windows,and locked doors, time and money slipping away.

On the twenty-seventh attempt, at ten-thirty in the morning, I turned the knob at Wells and Mines (I had been continuing to check the San Rafael office) and found that the knob turned. Heart in my throat, I opened the door. And there he was. Gold chains around his neck, diamond rings encrusted with gold or gold rings encrusted with diamonds on his fingers; he was wearing a fortune.

"Mr. Matucci," I said to him, after waiting five plus minutes for him to end a phone conversation. "I'm the guy with the legal paper."

He didn't say a word. He only extended his hand. I laid the paper in it. He gave me an exaggerated disgusted look, and I heeled around and exited.

As I was walking to my desk back at the office, Terry

informed me that Donald Washburn wanted me to call him. No doubt, Matucci had already called him.

"Hello, Mr. Washburn. I'm happy to report that finally, on the twenty-seventh attempt, I served, personally, Andy Matucci."

"Oh no, I wanted to stop you because he paid up in full. I wanted you to stop service."

"Gee, I'm sorry, the deed has already been done."

"Yes, I'm sorry, too but you know my client won't pay for your services now."

"Mr. Washburn, the bill is only twenty dollars, and you know, after twenty-seven times back and forth across the county, an accurate cost would be ten times twenty dollars and more."

"Well, we didn't want it served."

"We'll be billing you anyway. It's only fair."

"I'm still not paying. If I did, it would come out of my own pocket."

"You don't think all the effort I put in is worth something?"

"That's the way it is."

"Then I'll see you in small claims court."

And slam went the receiver on his end.

I put the phone down and glanced over at my partner. He smiled, "It goes with the territory."

Chapter 20

The Evasive Defendant

Once in a while, we work on a time and mileage basis. It has been our custom to charge twenty bucks an hour and thirty cents a mile. In such a case, there is no charge for the service itself. Some jobs demand the time and mileage charge, when, for example, the service is far away, very chancy and there is considerable urgency involved.

An attorney a few buildings from our office contacted us early one Monday morning, requesting fast action on serving four people in the South Bay. There was a court date for Friday of that week and the papers had to be served no later than Wednesday. The attorney knew it was going to be rough going. It was apparent that our twenty-five buck out of the county charge wasn't going to work so we went for time and mileage.

When the call came in, I was sitting at my desk, going over what little I had to do that morning. July was looking to be a very slow month. My $1,500 per month basic nut wouldn't be easy to crack. I had just gotten married that month, and considering the cost of the wedding and not working for a week, I knew it was going to be tight, so when Terry told me about the time and mileage job, I thought that it would at least get me through that one day.

Walking up to the attorney's office, I worried about money. The secretary went over the instructions on the serve. Three of the four persons to be served would probably be routine. The fourth person, a Daniel Tomchuk, the key defendant in the lawsuit, might be an evader.

Mulling things over on my way back to the office, I assumed there would be no problem. And the challenge that Tomchuk presented pleased me.

After making out the work sheets, I headed down to San Mateo in the Tercel. My son Vernon, on summer vacation from school, came with me. He was my shotgun, as usual, checking the map and asking questions. At age twelve, he was quite some help. Aware of the time and mileage situation, he would periodically lean over for a look at the odometer and announce how much we were making.

Highway 101, the big road that cuts through Marin, took me south past San Rafael, Larkspur and Greenbrae, Corte Madera, Mill Valley, Marin City and Sausalito. "Sausalito", by the way, was originally spelled "Saucelito" and was Spanish for "Grove of little willows." Warm summer mornings very often produced one of the most beautiful phenomena to be seen in Marin. On both sides of Waldo Grade at Sausalito, the heavy white billowing fog cascades down the mountain from the ocean to the other side and gently crashes onto the roadway. Fog is never lovelier. Sometimes it is too warm for the fog to roll all the way down the hill, so it appears to cap the coastal hills with a foamy mantle. Driving to or from the City in the morning or evening in the hot months may afford a view of the cloudy torrent. By mid-day, however, the fog river dries up. On this day, the land was still cool enough to allow the fog to advance all the way down to the highway. My windshield attracted enough moisture to necessitate use of the wipers.

20 – The Evasive Defendant

First on the list was the owner of an insurance agency and his wife. Easy enough. He was at his desk and friendly. After giving him the paper, I asked for help in serving his wife. He readily complied and gave me instructions on where his wife was working. Again, easy enough. The wife smiled and even said "Thank you," as I handed her the paper.

The next job was to deliver a court order to a blind man. There was a cover letter that our attorney client had sent with the legal documents, which, up to that point, I had not read thoroughly. But the blind man activated my curiosity, so I began to peruse the papers, hoping to discover the nature of the lawsuit. Early in my process serving career, I would read most of the complaints. Later on, I would occasionally read the ones that looked interesting. But after a while, it's, "If you've seen one, you've seen them all." However, this one was much different.

The basic story is that there was a default on a promissory note that the insurance agent and his wife had signed for. The amount was $79,000, a rather substantial sum. Not a penny had been paid back on the principal or the interest. It got better. An apartment complex had been purchased with the $79,000, and two additional loans totaling $128,000 had been obtained using the apartment building as collateral, somehow. Again, not a penny had been paid. And the new money had been used to buy two more apartment complexes right in the same area as the first one. The blind man was the rent collector for all the properties, and he was turning the money over to Daniel Tomchuk, who was the investor who had put the deals together for the insurance agent and wife. No wonder Tomchuk was the key man.

The blind man lived in one of the apartment buildings under consideration. My job was to read an order to him, saying he was no longer to collect any rents and/or turn any money over to Tomchuk. Vern went into the apartment with me to check it all out himself. He had no trouble understanding what was up. It was fun talking the matter over with him. At his age, I hadn't been exposed to even a small fraction of what my son was already well acquainted with.

Having read the order to the rent collector, Vern and I left the very run-down apartment complex to begin the hunt for Tomchuk.

There were four addresses for Tomchuk—an apartment in San Carlos, a business in San Francisco, a P.O. box in San Francisco at Pier 39, and an address at the San Carlos Airport. We figured our best bet was the apartment. It took nearly an hour to find the place. A neat looking blonde about forty-five told me Tomchuk had never lived there and wanted to know how it was that I had her address for him. I, of course, didn't know. Weakly, I suggested that he might have been the former tenant, but she had lived there since the condo was build. Oh, well. At least it told me a little about Tomchuk.

Next, we decided to hit the airport. Though small, it was confusing. It was clear the thing was mainly used for small aircraft. When I asked for Tomchuk at the administration office, everybody seemed to know him. Turned out he was a regular there and owned a plane which was in one of the hangers. I even got the hanger number from a secretary there. Before I left the office, a mechanic walked in and told me he had just seen Tomchuk drive away in his van not more than five minutes earlier. He'd probably been warned about someone looking for him. The mechanic told me what make and color the van was. He even told me a Rolls Royce and a Harley Davidson motorcycle were parked in the hanger, along with Tomchuk's Cessna. As I began to walk away, the mechanic followed after me.

"How do you like working on planes?" I asked him.
"Oh, I like it. Good money, too."
"You get lots of business?"
"Sure, especially now that everyone wants to fly."
"You do any work for Dan?"
"Sure. I'm working on his now. He wants me to have it ready by six tomorrow."
"By six? Think you'll make it?"
"Easy, just a few more hours."
"Where's Dan headed?"
"Chicago. But first to Tucson."
"You do a lot of work for Dan?"
"Yeah, quite a bit. I work on his boat, too."
"Right, at Pier 39."
"Yeah."
"He's got some boat."
"It's a yawl or a ketch, I never get straight on which is which."
"What's that boat's name?"
"Dan's Home. He lives on it, you know."
"Yeah, right."

Vern was walking with us the whole time and he could barely hold it in. As soon as the mechanic headed back toward the hanger, he burst out with a few praises. "Dad, that was great. We've really got him now."

"Hope so, Vern. Let's head for Pier 39 and check out that boat."

We found out from the harbormaster that Dan's Home was on dock J, slip 12. Though we had no key to the gate and therefore couldn't get on the dock itself, we walked over to see what we could see.

Dan's Home turned out to be a fifty-foot yawl worth at least a fortune. Vern guessed the berth cost as much a month as our house did. Daniel, the investor, was collecting a lot of rent, all free and clear. I began wondering what kind of power he had over the insurance agent and his wife. The entire operation had been going on for slightly more than a year. Somewhere, a slick lawyer must have been involved to enable Tomchuk to get away with the scam so long.

Vern and I were figuring out how to get over the gate when a healthy looking woman with a see-through blouse walked over and offered to open the gate for us.

"Hi. You need in?"

"Sure do."

"Well, here's in."

She was pretty bombed and the way she looked at me, I knew she was thinking interesting thoughts.

Reaching out, I held her arm. "Thanks very much. You're very lovely."

"I have a boat, too, next dock, first slip on the left. Come on over anytime."

"Thanks again."

She picked up my left hand and felt the ring on my finger.

"Oh, that's all right. You know where I'm at."

"Yes, I do."

Vern caught it all and he was nudging me as the woman bounced off toward her dock. He was becoming interested in all kinds of new things at age twelve.

Feeling like slick detectives, we checked out Dan's Home. No one was onboard. We grabbed a coke and fries at one of the places on the Pier, spending an hour and tried again. But still nothing. We were able to come and go on the dock because we used a splinter of wood to keep the wire gate door propped open just a hair.

Unhappily, we were already in commute time, so we decided to wait until around seven. Sitting at the far end

20 – The Evasive Defendant

of the dock, we took off our shoes and splashed our feet in the not too polluted bay water. When it began to cool down, we called it quits. I had to get Vern home, but a decision had to be made. Would I come back later that night and "sit on" Tomchuk, or would I be at the San Carlos Airport early that next morning?

My decision to try the boat again was prompted by the distance from my house to the San Carlos Airport. Pier 39 is one third as far. After a quick dinner and a look at the mail, I jumped in my machine again. In half an hour, I was on the dock walking to Dan's Home. Not a light shone; not a sound could be heard on the long white sailboat. Daniel was a real mover, I knew, so I thought I'd wait until midnight anyway. Fixing myself up with French fries and coffee, I seated myself behind the wheel of Dan's Home. At every sound of the gate rattling, I jumped up and climbed out of the boat. I felt it wouldn't look good to be caught lounging on the craft.

It was not an altogether unpleasant experience, waiting on the yacht. The lights of the wharf blazed away, and people were scurrying all along the walkways and streets. Cars crept along the Embarcadero, but the water was black and quiet and peaceful.

There was no wind and no clouds. There were stars without a moon, boats rocking on the tiny swells, a time for thinking and reviewing. Daniel Tomchuk never showed up.

It was a short night since I was up at four readying myself for the trip to San Carlos. I got my granola out, heated up some coffee, poured a thermos full of orange juice, and I was off. The Tomchuk thing was getting to me, as I now wanted him very badly. This would be my last shot.

Heading into the airport at 5:10 AM, a two-prop job, a Bonanza, passed directly overhead. An odd time for a private plane to take-off, I thought. The deserted parking lot made it easy for me to park in such a way as to be able to see Tomchuk's hanger. There was no activity anywhere. The only movement was a revolving search light atop a tower near where I was parked. The stab of light cut across my car every twenty seconds. For the first few minutes, I jumped every time the light hit the car.

Tomchuk's mechanic had said he would take-off at six. Many times, it had crossed my mind that the mechanic had either lied to me or had talked with Tomchuk about the guy who'd questioned him. That disturbing possibility bore in on me more and more as the time slipped away.

At 6:15, I got out of the car and walked to the hanger. Tomchuk's van was parked right beside it. That was a bad sign. There was enough light for me to look into the hanger. Through a sizeable slit in the door, I could see the Rolls, the Cessna, and the Harley. That was fine, but why the van?

Not wanting to go back to the car, I walked around the place. A guy rolled by in a service vehicle and asked me what I was doing. Honesty was best in the situation, I felt, so I explained I was looking for Tomchuk. He told me Tomchuk showed up at the coffee shop at 7:30 every morning, almost without fail.

I was feeling pretty low. At twenty bucks an hour, I was rolling up a large bill, but it wouldn't satisfy unless the job was completed successfully. At least, I thought, I'd wait until 7:30 to see if Tomchuk would show at the coffee shop.

Precisely on time, I walked into the tiny restaurant. The waitress spoke to me the second I crossed the threshold.

"You looking for Dan Tomchuk?"

"Yes."

"He told me to tell you he took off at 5 AM."

She gave me a superior smile.

"Looks like I missed him, but he didn't take his Cessna."
"Oh, he borrowed a friend's Bonanza."
"Right."

When I got back on 101 heading north, I found out something I'd never known before. The commute traffic gets heavy twenty miles south of San Francisco.

Chapter 21

Sooner or Later

There are some people on whom I can't wait to serve papers. Evading is anyone's prerogative, but there are times when I'll stop at very little to track down a person.

Very near our office is a small manufacturing plant, which is sued on a regular basis. It is run by a nice enough guy who always accepts the papers cordially when I finally corner him. It's his receptionist who stirs me up. Every time I go into the place, I run into her, since she is positioned behind a desk in the front lobby.

"Is Mr. Garibaldi in?"
"No, he's not come in yet."
"When will he be in?"
"In an hour."
"Thank you."
I smile and leave. But I'm back in an hour.
"Is Mr. Garibaldi in?"
"Yes, but he's in a conference."
"When will he be free?'
"About noon."
"Thank you."

At noon, I step up to the desk.
"Is Mr. Garibaldi in?"
"No, he's left for lunch."
"Will you give him my card and ask him to call me?"
"I'll give it to him when he comes back from lunch."
"Thank you."
I am so polite. I'd like to strangle her.
Of course, there is no call. Next morning, I call.
"Hello."
"Hello, is Mr. Garibaldi in?"
By now, she knows my voice.
"No, he won't be in till later."
"Will you ask him to call me?"
"Oh yes, as soon as he comes in."
Next morning, I try again.
"Mr. Garibaldi is in conference."

That's good enough for me – he is probably there. Quickly, I jump into the car and roll over to the place. As I park, I can feel myself getting irritated. As usual, Miss Wonderful is behind her desk.

"Is Mr. Garibaldi in?"
"No, he hasn't come in yet."
"You just told me over the phone that he was in conference."

For the first time in a dozen or so encounters, she was nearly ready to drop the façade and scream at me. It was a delicious moment. I smiled sweetly down at her.

"You do know if he's in or out?"

I was taking advantage, and I was going for more when Mr. Garibaldi himself walked into the lobby, wiping his glasses clean with a tissue. Deftly, quickly, I drew the order of examination from my shirt pocket, opened it up and flapped it in front of his face.

"This is for you." Putting his glasses back on, he stared

at the paper, grimaced, took it from me, whirled around and disappeared into the interior of the building.

I was very pleased and sported a huge smile on my face as I opened the front door and looked back briefly at the receptionist.

"Thank you."

This story has a bit of a P.S. The very next day, Terry held up a summons and complaint for me to see. "Here's another one for Garibaldi."

I wasn't pleased. It meant hassle, frustration, and more crap from that receptionist.

Of course, I had to try, even though I would have preferred to skip it. I walked in, told that woman I had a legal paper for Garibaldi, and waited for the lies. Instead, she picked up the phone, punched two lights, told someone a process server had a legal paper. Not a word to me, not even a sideways glance. She made her call and turned to her typewriter. A moment later, Garibaldi himself walked in, held out his hand and I put the paper in it.

Later, while talking with Terry, he was able to put the situation into perspective. Garibaldi and his receptionist had given up. They were convinced I'd get them sooner or later. We'll see.

Chapter 22

The Jerk Deserves a Serve

Problem serves offer a special challenge. Number one in that category, my absolute favorite, was one in which the defendant was clearly evading and had also cheated the plaintiff in a blatant manner. In this case, the plaintiff had paid seven hundred dollars up front to a photographer to shoot his wedding, but the photographer had never shown up and would not return the seven hundred.

The defendant, a Dick Arnold, was a guy Terry and I had served before, and neither one of us respected him. He lived in a great wooden mansion on E. Strawberry, Mill Valley; locals call the area Strawberry Point. And it was a mansion—decks, rock walls, pillars and wrought iron gates, leaded windows, even some real stained glass. Though I couldn't see them, I'm sure there was a pool and a hot tub, maybe more. There was a Grange debris box off the driveway, indicting some kind of work in progress. I could see Arnold was one of Marin's finest. And I knew where he was getting some of his money.

It was a small claims paper with the plaintiff going after his lost seven hundred, basing his claim on a breach of contract. A small claims action has a court date and must be served at least seven days prior to that date for a personal serve, which it would have to be, since Arnold lived alone.

With seven days left, I still hadn't gotten Arnold. The plaintiff had made several anxious calls to me during the month I'd been trying. In one call, he told me how upsetting it was for him and his wife having only a few instamatic shots of their wedding. Here was a chance to be involved in righting a wrong. The road to Arnold's house lead me past Golden Gate Baptist Theological Seminary, where I had graduated with a Master of Divinity degree. Arnold was not a potential convert, and I wasn't intending to minister to him at all. I hoped none of my old professors would disapprove that I wanted to be a good process server and get the bum Dick Arnold.

But I couldn't figure out Arnold's schedule. He didn't fall for the phony appointments I tried to set up either. I talked to him four or five times, always using my fictitious name. It was hard to tell if he was irresponsible and lazy or whether he suspected me. At the outset, I even agreed to five hundred dollars for him to photograph my wedding. Time after time, he failed to show up as planned.

And Arnold seemed to never go home. Early, late, very early, very late, I never caught him home. From a neighbor, I learned he drove a green Mercedes and always parked in his garage, which had a remote-control door. That meant that I could pound and pound on the door and get nowhere. Also, with a house the size Arnold lived in, he could be home and it wouldn't be apparent.

When I was down to the last day, I decided to park blocking Arnold's garage and write a story for this book and just wait. I had some coffee, some blueberry granola, and a missionary zeal deep in my little black heart.

22 – The Jerk Deserves a Serve

One hour, two hours, nearly three, and a green Mercedes was coming down the street. I knew it was Arnold when the driver pulled up behind me and gave me a "What the hell are you doing?" gesture.

There was a danger he'd drive off, so I wanted him to get out of his car. I pretended I was having trouble starting my car. Twice, I turned the ignition on and switched it off. That was enough. Arnold got out of his car and walked up to me. The window was down and the paper ready.

"All right jerk, what are you doing here?"

Ah, a tough guy.

"Oh, excuse me. Is this your place?"

"Let's move it."

"Sure."

His "jerk" riled me up. Slowly, I climbed out of my car. We were a good match in terms of age and size.

"You know what this is, jerk? This is a legal paper, jerk. A guy wants his money back. You knew if you didn't show up to photograph my wedding you'd be in deep shit, jerk."

With those well-chosen words, I let the pink sheet flutter to the ground.

"Get your green machine out of my way."

With considerable pleasure, I called the plaintiff and let him know he needed to be ready for his court date. I wished him good success.

Chapter 23

Beach and an Easy Serve

I save the Stinson Beach and Bolinas serves for sunny days, if I can. It is hardly worth it to drive to either town to make twenty-five or thirty bucks. But one such serve takes care of the gas for a trip to the beach.

Stinson Beach is not a bad place to have serves. The streets are well laid out and the people are regular folk, home a lot, accessible, not usually too paranoid. Bolinas, however, is the reverse. The streets are confusing, often not on the map, and weirdness and paranoia run as high as the flood time. Though not always true, Bolinas is a good place to hide for people who are being sued and often don't want to be found.

Lisa, Vern and I headed out to Stinson one Saturday, and I intended to make an attempt to serve a woman in Bolinas. It was a small claims paper from a well drilling company. My guess was that the floods of 1981-1982 had ruined a well and a new one had been needed – drilled, but not paid for. Simple enough, but first, fun in the sun.

Growing up in Los Angeles, I had learned to appreciate Southern California beaches. There is a distinct northern flavor to Stinson: yellow sand, a long, wide beach, lots of

23 – Beach and an Easy Serve

people on a sunny day, surf boards, beer, bikinis—rather like some of the beaches on which I'd hunted girls in my high school days. But the water and air temperatures are not as warm. Few take headlong rushes to dive into the surf at Stinson.

We spread out our blanket, put the 'Playmate' cooler on one end, the picnic basket on another to foil the wind, and piles of clothes on the other two corners, and we were there. That's another difference; wind is rarely a factor down south.

Lying at the beach, I was on my way to work. That's typical of the job—on the way to a movie, out to dinner, home from church—there was always a stop.

"You guys, I've got a couple stops to make."

"Oh, no" comes the chorus, every time.

"Okay, how many this time?"

"Just a couple, right on the way."

Vern expects it now and won't believe me when I say I haven't any to serve.

"Come on, Dad, how many do we have to do?"

And lying on the beach, I hadn't told Lisa and Vern we had to go to Bolinas yet.

It was the first week of August. Lisa and I had been married for one month, and it was a lovely day. The water was too cold for Lisa and me but not for Vern. He'd periodically run up to us from the beach and fling sizzling cold water on our sunburns. The beach was crowded, frisbees flying through the air, girls with nice tans and bodies to match paraded by, and guys with spa muscles did the same. It was a pleasant way to spend an afternoon.

Before leaving Stinson, we walked over to the little snack shack and got us some ice cream cones. I've often thought how nice it would be to own such a place.

While we were walking back to the car eating the ice

cream, I let it out that I had to make a run up to Bolinas to serve a paper. Surprisingly, there was no static, simply two "Okay"s.

On the way from Stinson to Bolinas, I asked Lisa to look up the street I wanted. After turning the Thomas map pages for a few miles, she found the street was not listed. That sounded like Bolinas. A made-up street no doubt that would not appear on any map, since it was a creation of a local citizen. In such a case, the solution is to ask around downtown.

We took the first turn off to Bolinas, the southernmost, and the first stop sign we came to was adjacent to the large nursery on the Olema-Bolinas Road and Mesa Road. Stopping there, we wondered which way to go. The bulk of the Bolinas population lives on the Mesa, but information might be easier to come by in the town. As I was making up my mind, Lisa spotted the road we wanted directly across from us. Nailed on a tree was a homemade street sign. There it was, right in front of us. It was déjà vu, miracle, surprise, all rolled into one.

Happy and amazed, I drove along the pitted dirt road. There were no house numbers visible, so I decided to stop at a likely house and ask for the party I wanted. I pulled into a driveway, walked up to the door and knocked. Standing there, I looked back and smiled at Lisa and Vern waiting in the car. I was hoping I wasn't going to have to cart them all over the Bolinas Mesa maze.

A nice-looking woman opened the door.

"Hi, I'm lost, I think. Can you tell me where Eleanor John lives?"

"I'm Eleanor John. Do I know you?"

The feeling I'd gotten when we spotted that street sign on the tree came again, this time stronger.

"Now you won't believe this, but I have a legal paper for you."

"You don't mean it."

"I do, in fact. Here it is."

I hauled it out of my shirt pocket, unfolded it and handed it to her. When Eleanor reached for and took the paper, I heard a muffled cheer from the occupants of the little white car parked in the drive.

"You know, Eleanor, it is kind of amazing how I found you. Complete accident. Actually, I drove right here and this street of yours isn't even on the maps."

"That's real amazing. Who are you?"

"My name's Kent. The people who drilled the well are clients of mine. I'm a process server."

"They never drilled any well. After the flood, I needed a new well and they just screwed everything up. Now they want money for nothing. They ain't gettin' a penny. Screw 'um."

"I hope everything works out. You probably have a good defense. Get all your facts together and argue it out in court. If you don't show up, you'll lose and who knows what will happen."

"Screw 'um."

"Right. But if you ignore it all, you'll probably be the one to be getting screwed. You know a lawyer? That's the best thing to do. Lay out the real facts and get an opinion. Then you'll know."

"I'll try that, those bastards. I finally got water just last week. I ought to sue them."

"Might be a good idea if they promised you a well. Anyway, check it out and good luck."

I had a real satisfied feeling as I drove back down that awful route to the Bolinas-Olema Road. A day at the beach, thirty bucks, a tough and distant serve out of the way, and a touch of the unusual had fallen upon us.

Chapter 24

Feast or Famine

"You guys are going to drive me to bankruptcy."
"It's getting to be tough, I guess. Lots of people in your spot. I see it every day. There's no way I cannot give you this paper, though. If I chose not to, to try to help you, the sheriff would do it instead of me, and I'd maybe lose my client. And I can't afford that. Besides, think of the gas and the time. I've made four trips up this hill."

The road in question was scenic in San Anselmo, a windy one up the side of a hill that was not fun to drive. The guy I was talking to was a contractor who hadn't been able to pay a materials bill, because he needed that money to cover himself in other areas. Quite common. And it wasn't evil for the suppliers to want to get paid. Marin isn't that big, and a contractor could get blacklisted if he didn't pay for his materials. That would be his end then.

There was nothing funny about the bankruptcy talk, either. I've seen business after business go under. And the reasons, whether in good times or bad, can be summarized thus: high interest, inflation, and taxes. And the result is that people become afraid, and the fear causes them to not spend, not pay, and sue for debts more quickly than they normally would. Times are bad, not 'Grapes of Wrath' bad, but bad enough to produce a booming process serving business. In a direct way, during the economic slump, the work picked up, and thus I have profited because others are suffering. Of course, there is no reason for process servers to turn down business or start making value judgments on which papers they'll serve. I ride the wave.

I don't know how wrong it is to avoid paying debts. We have to eat and live. Many people have been forced to simple living: no credit buying, cash only. If you don't have it, you don't do it. The problem is that recessions follow good times, and in the good times, we climb out on a limb, overextend, and the ego and the goal of financial security takes a beating.

Perhaps we get more honest in a recession. The affluent, who got that way due to questionable tactics, are trimmed back to reality. They lose their houses, cars, investments, gold chains, fancy offices, and some friends. But their nasal passages can heal, more time can be spent at home with the family; books and the radio can be rediscovered, and the Giants can become an exciting baseball team. The poor are not necessarily happier; it is not good or fun to be poor. It is good to be content with what we have. An observant process server learns to be a bit of a philosopher.

People rarely starve anymore. I've never missed more than a meal or two and that was usually because I was too busy to stop. My parents missed meals; my grandparents missed a great many meals, and there was no back up. Out in the Sand Hills of Nebraska, my roots, there was no welfare in the twenties and thirties and forties, and if times were bad, people starved. Neighbors shared what they had. Often, especially during prolonged drought, there wasn't much to share. So, people packed up and searched for work, food, and shelter. Sometimes they found it; once in a while, they didn't. Kids died first, always. My folks made it to the shipyards in Portland, Oregon and the canneries in Carlton and Forest Grove. They never went to a government office for charity, even when they could have. Today, in bad times, we don't pay bills, and we run into bankruptcy and then the civic center. I'm not any different. The system shakes a little, but the system endures. We won't change now. We don't have to now. If we changed, I'd be out of a job.

Chapter 25

Tricks or Treats?

There is a story about a process server who attended a wedding and served the minister with a small claims paper after the ceremony. From a close friend, I heard about the head of a school board being served in the very midst of a board meeting. The client had asked the server, on promise of extra pay, to do his best to embarrass the defendant.

At a propitious moment, this colleague of mine walked to the floor microphone during a rather heated debate as though he was going to speak on the issue.

"Mr. Sinclair."

The board chairman said, "Yes, go on."

"Mr. Charles Sinclair."

"Yes, yes. What is it?"

"This paper I have in my hand is a summons and complaint. You have been sued, and you have thirty days to make an answer to the court on this debt you owe and have refused to pay."

I want it understood that I was not the one who did this. Of course, I might have done it had the opportunity been mine.

I did take advantage of Halloween once. A woman who worked for a large self-help kind of secular cult would not open her door. A secretary shielded her at the group's headquarters, and the client did not want to put out money for a stakeout. Since it was mid-October, I put the paper away for trick-or-treat night.

Vern went along with me, looking forward to it really. He marched up to the door in his pirate's outfit after I'd positioned myself appropriately. He knocked; the defendant opened the door; Vern said, "Trick-or-treat." A candy bowl was offered; Vern took a few pieces, said "thank you," and stepped back, and I took his place.

"Trick-or –treat yourself. Here's your paper and you are served. I guess you thought you'd beaten me. You didn't. Have a good night."

In Mill Valley, or really Strawberry, is a major condo complex on Harbor Drive. There is a large, beautiful pool, an outdoor hot tub, tennis courts, and a spacious clubhouse with a bar, card room, televisions, pool tables and decks. It is very nice indeed. And there are lots of young singles, especially females, using the pool during the weekdays.

Singles who live in condos are not always easy to serve; they're often out, using their place only to sleep in. I had a dissolution of marriage paper for a guy who lived in one of the Harbor Drive condos. For weeks, I had tried without success. I was there early and late, weekdays, weekends— nothing. I could see into the kitchen and tell someone was living there, and someone was reading both the Chronicle and the Independent Journal.

One hot Wednesday afternoon, while trying to serve the defendant in Strawberry, I happened across a neighbor of the guy I wanted, who told me I could find him at the pool. It was a quickie conversation, and I couldn't get a description.

I believe in dressing comfortably and I had on shorts, but I also had my swimsuit on underneath. That is common practice for me in the summer. I'll bet I hold a record for swimming in more pools in Marin than anyone else. Over to the pool I went, and there was no doubt as to whom it was I wanted. In the middle of the pool were several girls and one guy. They were playing with a huge yellow rubber duck, climbing onto it, sliding off, pushing and touching each other, seemingly oblivious to anything else. My defendant was a good-looking guy in his mid-thirties; the girls were a bit younger, and it was fun time. Their drinks and beers were sitting on the edge of the pool, to which they made frequent trips.

Sitting in a white plastic deck chair, I surveyed the situation. My first inclination was to swim out with the paper, but no, it would have gotten wet. That would have been the most fun, though. Second best would have been to call the guy over to me and serve him privately. Or, I could situate myself near the drinks and get him when he came over to sample his shooter.

But, I was hot and in need of relaxation, so I took off my shoes, shorts and shirt and dove into the pool. The guy couldn't get away, I knew; therefore, I might as well enjoy myself a while.

Swimming around, I caught the attention of one of the ladies who swam after me and dunked me as I made a pass close by the yellow duck. In a few minutes, I too, was fooling around with the group. It was quite a good deal of fun. The defendant and I even exchanged some small pleasantries. I could tell he wasn't happy to have lost the undivided attention that he had been enjoying from the girls. He gave me a "how are you, you creep" look.

Everyone was well on their way to being smashed and I could foresee what might be going on in a bedroom or two in the near future. Being an engaged man, I'd determined to pass on it and stick to business.

It was in the transition from pool to bedroom that I made my move. Hopping out of the pool, I asked my man if I could talk to him a minute. While the girls were pushing the rubber duck out of the pool, I slipped the legal paper to a very surprised person. He looked at the paper, looked at me, and gave out a big whoop of excitement. Rushing to show the girls the paper, he was shouting that his wife was finally divorcing him. I wasn't expecting that reaction.

Though I'd at first been accepted by the girls, their opinion of me changed immediately. Certainly, they felt betrayed, and in a way, they were right. I was sporting around with them only because I wanted to serve a legal paper. I'd tricked them. I'd been a good process server. You can't please everyone for sure. But the defendant wasn't angry at me; he simply ignored me. He was probably relieved that I was no longer a threat to him in regard to the girls. And actually, it couldn't have been better for him. Here was clear proof that he was going to be single soon, and it was presented by an independent source. I was discredited in front of the women, while he had been catapulted onto the top of the heap.

There was nothing for me to do but leave. The sun was drying me off as I walked to my little pile of clothes. I pulled my shorts up over my wet suit, pulled on my shirt and stepped into my tennis shoes. Without tying the shoes, I started for the parking area. As I walked over the last stretch by the pool, I stopped, slowly tied my shoes and watched the group from which I'd so recently been excluded. One of the girls caught me eyeing them and, much to my surprise, gave me a nice smile and a tiny wave.

Chapter 26

Is It Worth Getting Shot?

The biggest rush to serve a paper is reserved for a TRO, a Temporary Restraining Order, especially when the plaintiff is in some kind of jeopardy from the defendant. And a TRO is by far the serve with the greatest potential of danger for the server.

Usually, a TRO is issued to prevent domestic violence. My first TRO involved a parent/child situation. The parents were the plaintiff and their eighteen-year-old son, who was coming home drunk and beating up on mom and dad, was the defendant. I served the young man at his friend's house where a small gang of kids was working on motorcycles and beer. Fortunately, I caught them at just the right time, when they were still mellow and not yet mean.

Among my favorite TRO serves is the one that involved a wife as plaintiff and a husband as defendant, a TRO by means of which the wife wanted to prevent the estranged husband from sailing off to Hawaii on the family yacht with the eighteen-year-old girlfriend. I caught the guy as he was rigging his boat. He looked at the paper I'd handed him, and his little sweety bounced over for a gander too. Then, while she did the holding, he did the lighting, and half consumed by flames, the TRO was dropped into the sea. As I sat on the dock filling out the worksheet, the boat was readied for sailing. Driving away, I looked back to see the boat reach the end of the harbor and move into the Bay proper for its run under the bridge and westward.

Another vivid memory of a TRO serve was when I handed one to a woman in her mid-sixties, a regular housewife type with grandchildren, whose husband of thirty-nine years had left home to be with his new girlfriend and his bottle. He was having a TRO served on his wife to prevent her from selling the family home. I stood on the porch while the lady read the document. Understandably, she fell apart as she realized what the paper meant. For over an hour, I sat with the woman while she poured out a tragic story. All I did was listen and try to comfort her. After most of the tears were mopped up, I helped her figure out a lawyer to consult. The serve of the TRO was the first contact with a legal matter she had had in her entire life.

To date, though, one TRO serve stands head and shoulders above all others. Setting the scene is easy enough. A man in his early fifties, a big guy and a hard drinker, had moved in with a same-aged woman he'd met in a bar. As far as I could tell, they were drinking buddies. She lived in a beautiful home in the Peacock Gap area of San Rafael. He was without a job, car, and money, but he had been able to sweet-talk this little lady. And for a year plus, they'd been together. In that time, she'd picked up a broken collarbone, a broken forearm, numerous cracked ribs, and her face had taken a lot of punches. Still, they carried on until he went to work on the household furnishings. That was it; he had to go, so she went to a lawyer who typed up a TRO, filed it with the court, and tried to get it served.

The company that was asked to make the service did not get the job done, basically, as I understood, due to the intimidating efforts of the defendant and the seeming uncooperativeness of the plaintiff. It seems the lady would change her mind at the last minute and actually sick her boyfriend on any server who came to the door. A not-all-too-hard-to-understand story when drunks are involved. The lady had suffered, but she could not lose her co-alcoholic and lover. However, when the guy destroyed a very valuable vase collection and sold several expensive and cherished fur coats, the lady seemed angry enough to get serious about the TRO. And this time, her lawyer asked Terry and me to do the serving.

The plaintiff, Nina, called our office immediately after her lawyer had had the TRO dropped off at our office. I was to make the serve, and I felt I needed a description of the defendant, Fred, just in case. Fifty or so, he was big, over six feet tall and over two hundred pounds in weight. Usually, he was clean-shaven. He had black hair; at least what little hair he had was black. But he let one side grow long so he could comb it up and over his baldpate. And to get the hair to stay that way, he had it heavily greased. Nina told me he was home all day long and went out only in the evening to drink at various San Rafael Fourth Street bars. I knew which bars they would be, but I considered serving him at the house to be better.

For several days running, I tried. If he had been home, he never answered my knock. Glass from a broken front window littered the walk and driveway. The dents that Fred had made in Nina's Mercedes looked like expensive ones. I was hoping to avoid any such dents being inflicted upon me.

Day after day, I made the rather long trip to Nina's. On several occasions, Nina answered the door only to tell me Fred was sleeping and couldn't come to the door. My partner and I discussed the matter and figured that we were dealing with a sick situation. Nina seemed to have a neurotic need for Fred and his behavior, and at the critical point, really didn't want him out. Nina's attorney thought I was crazy when I told him what we felt. Terry and I wanted the lawyer to know I wasn't going to make one more trip unless I had Nina's full cooperation. The attorney told me then to let the serve go. It was obvious the attorney didn't like my interference, but enough was enough. We had no doubt lost another client.

A week or so later, we got a call from Nina's lawyer. Fred had broken Nina's arm again and she wanted Fred out desperately. Okay, but we set some demands down. We wanted Nina to be present and to usher Fred to me, but with a San Rafael cop in attendance as well.

From time to time, a police officer has been asked to be present for a serve. It is called a "civil standby." Police departments don't like to do it, but will if they can fit it in. And you have to have a good reason for such a request and potential violence usually does it.

A rendezvous was set up. Six o'clock Friday evening, a cop would meet Nina and me two blocks from the house. Nina would go to the door and knock until Fred opened up. I would be off to one side; the cop would be somewhere behind me. Nina was right on time and eager to get on with it. The cop, however, was not cooperative at all and was in an ugly mood. He wouldn't let me explain the situation and refused to listen to our plan. Nina was fairly drunk, too.

Anyway, it was the best I could do and there wasn't going to be a second time for me. My personal plan was to go along with it, but at the first sign of trouble, I was going to be gone.

Nina pulled her car into the driveway. I parked two houses ahead, on the far side of the street. The cop parked his black and white directly in line with the front door. Nina stumbled her way to the door; I positioned myself just to the left of the door; the cop lounged against the passenger side of his car smoking a cigar. The TRO was rolled like a baton in my right hand, ready to pass to Fred the minute I spied his greasy head.

Nina knocked over and over. No response. She called, "Fred, Fred open up honey."

That got him. He flung the door open, yelling at the top of his lungs at her. Nina retreated and Fred staggered out, fell as he did so, and landed right at my feet.

The cop remained where he was. Nina slipped into her house and slammed the door. I helped Fred up, unrolled the paper, reading pertinent parts to him, especially the part where he was to leave immediately taking only his personal belongings. He listened to me silently and when I'd finished, he grabbed the paper out of my hand. In a few seconds, the paper was torn into little pieces. Fred glared at me but said nothing. Instead, he attacked the door, beating on it and yelling for Nina. Seeing the violent scene about to erupt, I looked for our cop. He was just pulling away as I did.

Nina, true to my opinion, opened up for Fred and rushed into his arms. As soon as Fred saw he had that situation under control, he turned his attention to me.

I was not pleased. For one thing, I was going to charge Nina's attorney a bundle, and I was not about to run off by a sloppy, greasy Fred.

With Fred billowing his rage at me, I walked to the street. I'd already left my glasses in the Tercel. Planting my feet, I stood with my arms at my side. Fred advanced toward me, already swinging his fists. I would let him have the first shot, but as soon as he came within striking distance, he stopped and began hurling all kinds of vulgarisms at me. He shouted; I was silent, waiting.

"Get off my street."

I was silent.

"Get off or I'll beat the hell out of you."

"Get on with it Fred; I'm going to put you in the hospital."

"The hell you will."

"Take your punch, Fred, come on you bald jerk. Take your punch."

"I'm going to kill you, you bastard. I'll shoot your ass."

He ran back to the house. Nina, who'd been watching, told me he had a gun in the house. That was all I needed to hear. To hell with Nina, I thought, at least I'm not going to get shot. I ran to my car and rolled away.

Monday morning, I called the attorney and give him the rundown. He listened and said to send him the bill. We requested double the normal charge, but it should have been double that.

It's been two months now and no check. In another month, if there is still no pay, we'll take the attorney to small claims court. It shouldn't be too difficult to win a judgment.

Chapter 27

Will the Real Clara Please Stand Up

Sausalito has some impossible streets. With the name Central Avenue, one wouldn't think it was one of the worst. I can never find it without the aid of my Thomas map. There is a Central in Woodacre, and there it is; there is a Center in San Anselmo and Fairfax, and they are, too, pretty much. Novato has a Center, a long street that cuts through the main residential area; San Rafael has a Center in its West End area above Fifth, and maybe it used to be; even Mill Valley has a Central, but it isn't even close.

Sausalito's Central is one way, no doubt because the road is so narrow. When I find it, I'm often at the wrong end and am forced to find the good end. This is not easy, and a time or two, I've given up. I live by a simple maxim – never attempt a serve on Central at night when it's raining. This rule is worthy of considerable attention.

One bright summer Saturday morning, I got up the courage to find Central in Sausalito. I'd been holding the paper for a month or more before I'd made even the first attempt. The defendant was a Clara Price. She owed money on a used car that she'd financed through on of the local banks. Balancing the paper on the steering wheel, I read it as I drove down 101 toward Sausalito. Clara had paid back half the loan but hadn't made a payment for months. The issue seemed clear.

My map got me to Central after a very small increase in my pulse rate. I even located the address, which was on the far left side of a triplex. There was a full three-car parking space where there would have been a front yard, so I felt sure Clara would be home.

At first, I knocked lightly on the door. Then I knocked louder and longer. Then I rang the bell. Then I rang it again. A sizzle of frustration ran up my back and made sweat pop out on my forehead. I walked to the front window and peered in. I rapped on it and looked in again. There was no sound and no light, but the place felt warm. And it was Central in Sausalito, meaning I did not want to have to come back. If there had been a dog, I would have served the dog. But nothing.

Back in the car, I was reaching for my pen to note the diligence attempt when a very fat, short, middle-thirties woman suddenly appeared beside the car. She had on a pee green tent that was being used as a bathrobe.

"Hi," she said. "You were knocking at my door?"

"Looks like I should have waited longer. Yes, I was there. You must be Clara."

"No, no, you want to see Clara?"

"Yeah, for a minute. I need to see her. Is she home?"

"She's home. Do you want to come back down?"

"I'll be right there."

During the conversation, I was hiding the summons and complaint and the worksheet. I wanted the woman to walk away from the car so I could refold the paper and put it into my pocket. She did just what I'd hoped, and I was out following her, ready for the kill. At least, I would not have to come back to Central.

27 – Will the Real Clara Please Stand Up

There was a second woman inside all right, another huge one. The two could have easily passed for sisters. This one was lying on a couch, watching TV. A half dozen or so empty beer bottles were scattered around, as were assorted bags of chips and cookies.

"Hi Clara."

"What do you mean, 'Clara'? She's Clara."

The second fat one was pointing to the first fat one.

I turned to the latter, "Oh, you're Clara."

"Hell no, she is. What a lying bitch she is."

"Hey, you fat ass, you're the lying faggot."

One witty repartee followed closely on the heels of the other for some moments. At first, I thought it was a put-on, but I could see the air heating up.

"Okay now, ladies, who is Clara, because I have something important for the real Clara Price."

There was a pause in the action as the two looked at each other. I had already decided I was going to leave the paper with one or the other, but it would be best if I served the right person. Closely, I watched the expressions on the chubby faces, watched the eyes, and listened for clues.

"Come on girls, will the real Clara Price please raise her right hand."

They both raised the right hand and laughed at me.

One of the asked, "Who are you anyway?"

"I'm a process server. I've no personal interest in this. It'd really be great if you'd help me out."

"Why should we help you? Why don't you stick that paper where the sun never shines."

"What a wonderful suggestion. I'll try it if you tell me your name," I said to the one lounging amid the debris. But the other one piped up then, "She's Clara," and then I got, "No, she's Clara."

"One of you is Clara. You both look enough alike to be

sisters. Probably you are, so, Clara Price, you are served with this summons and complaint." I looked at both of them as I set the paper on the TV set. "And in thirty days, if there is no response, you'll be in default."

"You're trespassing. Out, get out, you creep, you parasite. I hate you damn bill collectors," said the one that had come out to the car. She seemed to be in control of the household and was no doubt the real Clara.

"I'm on my way. "It's been fun."

I had little doubt but that I'd get away with that one. If a motion to quash service of summons was filed and I did have to appear in law and motion court, I was sure a judge would uphold the serve.

Back in the car, I felt somewhat satisfied as I made out the worksheet. I wouldn't have to hunt for Central again for a while, hopefully. The next hour or so, I played mental games with myself on how I could have gotten the truth out of the big girls. Several possibilities came to mind. It was a case of knowing how, after it was too late. Process serving is like that; the tension of the moment often causes the mind to freeze up, and when you get fooled and fail to make the serve, you can get down on yourself. In the Clara Price serve, at best or at least, I had been only half off.

Chapter 28

Confident Is Better

When I first began serving, I was not very confident; too often I was embarrassed of my job, sometimes even ashamed. During that stage, I would make up various rationales for what I was doing.

"I work for the court," was a common lie I told. It seemed okay if I was from the court. People were sometimes even impressed. "Honey, a man from the court is here with a legal paper for you." It had a substantial sound to it. I used that one for months until one day I suffered considerable embarrassment over it and realized I had to stop.

It was a Fall Saturday morning, and I was driving west on Shoreline Highway past Tam Junction. The small claims paper was for a notorious evader whom I was told would lie about who he was.

Red Johnson was the defendant's name and when a redheaded man opened the door, there was little doubt I had my man.

"Hi Red."

"Yeah, what do you want?"

He said it in such a way that I was intimidated. The paper was in my back pocket, and it was going to be a chore getting it out. I rarely experience now what I did in the early months, and I can't explain exactly what went through me at such times, but it is a profoundly uncomfortable feeling. To counter my uneasiness, I said, "I'm from the court and I have a small claims paper for you."

"You're not from the court. Why do you have to lie about it? You're a crummy process server."

I was unable to respond.

"Gimmie the paper."

Still, I couldn't talk. It was like I'd been found out. But I managed to get the paper out and hand it over.

Red Johnson took the paper from my hand and slammed the door shut. Walking back to the car, I felt numb. I wanted to quit, punch Johnson in the face, swear at somebody, anything but serve another paper. Yet it was early in the day, my busiest day. On the seat of the car were a dozen or more serves to be done that morning. Oh, boy. And I was stripped of one of my hiding places.

There then followed a period of the use of self-effacing gestures and apologetic statements designed to make it plain that I was not a bad person.

"This just arrived on my desk yesterday and my job is to deliver it to you." This lie was received better than the court one, but I knew it was false and so must have others who were used to be being sued.

"Sorry I have to bring this out to you," was perhaps the worst of all. I said it with my hands in my pockets and my head down. Of course, I wasn't sorry, except on rare occasions. I was embarrassed about my job.

To be fair though, many serves were simply straight forward "gotcha's." I'd knock, ask for the defendant, receive a "Yes, that's me," and stick it in the person's hand and leave. But I was often jelly inside, only barely refraining from uttering an, "I'm sorry."

Now that I am a mature, truly professional process server, I handle each serve in a matter-of fact manner. It goes like this: "I have a legal paper, you are the defendant, here is the paper." And I walk away. Almost always. I've developed a new tactic if the situation allows. I stand and observe the reaction, for a smart remark, an explanation, a confession, an apology. Some put me in the place of judge and jury and begin a point-by-point argument of why the suit is absurd. A general denial is the proper term. Sometimes, genuine human pain or confusion is expressed in an emotional outburst. And I listen and make appropriate affirmations. Sometimes, I'll accept a cup of coffee, a beer, a martini; I sit and listen and say it will all be right. I always say, "Find a lawyer quick." It is not uncommon now to receive a handshake and a genuine, "Thank you."

It is clear that if I approach a serve in a confident manner, I'm in a better position to be a listener, perhaps a source of help, than if I were to approach the person to be served in an uneasy, apologetic manner. And I am much less likely to be pounced on by angry defendants. There is something about a lie, especially an "I'm sorry" that galls people. And as I coolly wait and watch a person react to a summons, I'm in a much better position to deck them if they should take a swing at me.

Chapter 29

God Sent Me

Bridgeway in Sausalito, the southernmost portion that runs right along the choppy Bay water, is my favorite strip of road of those in the populated areas of Marin. The buildings of San Francisco, with their lights along the paths of concrete, look very close when viewed from across the water. The City is more beautiful than London, Paris, even Venice.

Bufano's Sea Lion sculpture is a treat to see. Green and black with splotches of white (from birds), it is a landmark I always look for. When the tide is full, the water appears to be only a foot or two below the roadbed. Often, I've seen the black heads of seals bobbing up and down amidst the blue-green rolls of salt water. Like a schoolboy, I tell myself the water I see has been to Hawaii and back hundreds of times, and some of the sailboats have been there, too. Sometimes, I worry that I'll never make enough money process serving to get a boat of my own.

I had a small claims paper for a guy who lived in Sausalito's Hurricane Gulch. His big and beautiful three-tiered wood home was on Edwards Street. Here was another guy who lived in a half-million-dollar house who wouldn't pay a two-hundred-dollar bill for services rendered.

On the first two attempts, no one answered my knock, though lights shone throughout the massive structure. There are few things more irritating than that. And I pounded long and hard, ringing the bell over and over. Dead, drunk, or screwing, I thought, or stoned, or paranoid. Frustrated, it took the pleasure out of the homeward, northward drive along Bridgeway.

The third time was different. It was dark; daylight savings time had just given way to daylight wasting time; the first substantial fall rain was upon us, and no light shone from the house on Edwards. Given the results of my first visits, I should have simply turned around in the drive and rolled back the way I'd come, but I parked, tucked the thin pink summons into my pocket and walked to the door.

Standing at the base of the house, which rose over my head three full stories, I felt a chill of futility go through me. New wood, classic leaded windows, half a hill cut away, the smell of shingles and stain— all this I sensed as I stared at the black windows. But my knock on the massive oak door brought an immediate response; footsteps rapidly descended a carpeted stair, two flights up at least—bare feet, little feet, certainly not the guy I wanted.

The door swung open.

"Come in, come in, we've been waiting for you." A pretty woman, about forty and wearing classic Sausalito fashion stood there with her hand extended toward me. Without saying anything, I tried to put the summons into her hand. She seemed to not see it and obviously was intending to shake my hand. I did, too, the paper ending up between our palms. That was definitely a first for me. But as she released my hand, the paper was still in mine.

"Everyone is here, and we've already begun. The medium is in his trance and the spirit is speaking to us."

A séance. A mistake was being made.

"Oh, you're having a séance."

"Isn't that why you're here?"

"No, I came to see Peter Rust. He's here, right?"

"This is his house and he's upstairs now, but you can't interrupt the séance."

"I wouldn't want to do that."

Here was a dilemma. On the one hand, I wanted to serve the paper. Evidently, the woman who was standing there, waiting for me to make up my mind, didn't live there, so I couldn't sub her. Peter was in the séance. The idea of a séance scared me, because I knew about evil spirits. I knew the Old Testament condemned mediums, and the Christian Church taught that the medium's spirits were demons. And as a Christian, I believed it. My years as a street minister in the Haight-Ashbury had given me plenty of practical material substantiating the doctrine.

Greater than the fear I had of the unknown, even stronger than my desire to make a buck, I wanted to see what was up and, if possible, apply my faith to the situation. Quite a mixture of motives.

"Come on, what are you going to do?"

"I'll come up."

"You'll have to wait until the séance is over before you talk to Peter."

"Don't worry, I will."

We'd been talking on the very bottom set of stairs, standing in the darkness of the big house. I could see a flickering light above me that was being reflected in various windows and mirrors about me..

"Shh."

"Right."

Up we went, very slowly. At the second level, the smell of Indian incense hit me, the same smell I remembered from the Krishna Temple on San Francisco's Fredrick Street years before.

We climbed up into a large front room, glass on every

side, expensive rugs and fine furniture visible in the light of the lone candle provided. My eyes had already adjusted to the darkness, and I could clearly see the group gathered for the séance.

The medium, a thinnish man about thirty-five with a bushy moustache, was seated in a bulky wooden armchair. His shoes were off and he was speaking in a squeaky voice with his eyes closed and his hands clasped prayer style in front of him. There was only one other man present. He was about my age but with most of his hair gone. He was seated to the medium's left. Peter Rust, no doubt. There were also seven women.

Directly in front of the medium, sitting cross-legged on the floor were three of the women. And they were the youngest—one in her early twenties, one in her early thirties, one in her late thirties. To the right of the medium was a couch on which three more women sat. They all looked to be in their mid-fifties. The other woman, the one who had greeted me at the door, was seated right next to me, and we were behind the couch.

Everyone but the medium was dressed very well. The candlelight shone off many gold chains and diamonds. I was able to study each person unobstructed, since I was the only one open eyes. Every single face had a Buddha-like smile on it, but no one was trying for a lotus position. No one was even rocking back and forth Pentecostal fashion.

The medium was under the control of his familiar spirit, supposedly. For no less than thirty minutes, he rolled on and on about the universal religion. I caught some Hindu thought, Christian Science and Unity School of Christianity, a lot of reincarnation, some Edgar Cayce, EST and a bit of popular positive thinking thrown in. Round and round it went, with all the contradictions that aren't contradictions that are characteristic of esoteric eastern religion. Once in a while, one of the faithful emitted a "Hmmm" sound indicating approval. My prejudices were readily present with me. I had given up trying to be objective.

Finally, the monologue ended, and it was question and answer time. An interesting wrinkle, I thought.

One woman asked, "Tell me about the new relationship that has just become a part of my life."

There was a pause as the medium looked with closed eyes to the ceiling.

"Ah, my spirit is giving me something now. It's becoming clearer. Yes, this is really an old relationship just coming back into your life and even though you're attracted to him, you're afraid of the involvement."

"Oh no. I'm referring to a girl I've just hired at my business."

"Yes, yes. Let me seek the right level of the spirit. Yes, you are right, but what I said was true in a previous embodiment."

The woman seeking help from the spirit world said, "Oh, I see. Thank you so much."

I rolled my eyes and recrossed my legs.

Another episode of the same nature followed. The medium missed by a mile but cleared it up by invoking events that had transpired some lives earlier.

My favorite exchange, the one immediately prior to my own questions, was quite revealing. A bejeweled lady wanted help from the other side as to how to invest her money, a sizable sum, which she planned to invest soon.

The medium said he had to go deeper into his trance. For twenty or thirty seconds, he was silent.

"This one perplexes me. It is obvious this will require private sessions where more intense energy can be concentrated. Yes, yes, this must be handled in private sessions."

This medium was brighter that I'd given him credit for.

A few seconds pause in the proceedings encouraged me to venture a question of my own.

"What is your name, spirit?"

"Well now, I don't think I'll say."

"Are you an evil spirit?"

"Well now, what can I say?"

"Do you worship the devil?"

"Oh, I see, you're trying to test the spirits like Saint Paul said."

"Wrong again, Saint John spoke of testing the spirits. You aren't doing well tonight, are you Mr. Medium."

"Silence please, I'm leaving you now; everyone concentrate. Good byeeeee."

The candle was blown out by the woman who had let me in, and the room's lights were switched on. Everyone turned to look at me. One of the older women asked me who I was. I told her my name, even used the real one. Somehow, and I can't recall precisely how it happened, I ended up sitting in the medium's chair while he, silent all the while, sat on the floor in front of me. He was sipping on a glass of water someone had given him.

The most aggressive person, as it turned out, the one who wanted counsel on her investments, took control of the interrogation. Simply and slowly, I answered the questions. My feeling was that the so-called medium was swindling and deceiving. I wanted to poke a hole or two into his charade. I'd remembered the errors he had made during the question-and-answer time and how he had confused Paul and John. Surely a spirit from the other side, a spirit they were depending on for crucial answers, had to be considerably sharper. After a brief summation, I turned to the medium and said, "At first, I thought you were genuine. I do really believe in demon-controlled mediums, but I think it is more than clear that you are simply cheating these people."

He didn't say a word. He stood and walked into another part of the house, and that's the last I saw of him.

The investor had finally had enough and asked for a vote on whether or not to eject me. Some said I was sent from God, others said I was a born-again bigot. More of them said the latter.

After the vote, I asked Peter Rust to show me out. He was one who said God had sent me. We shook hands and got along well as we proceeded down two flights of stairs. At the bottom landing, I reached for my summons, soon to be his summons.

"Now Peter, you can see the mysterious fashion in which God has worked His will this time. I really came here to give you this legal paper."

With a smile, I drew the paper out of my left hip pocket and unfolded it. Peter couldn't believe it. His mouth fell open; his eyes grew wide, "A legal paper for me?"

"Yes, Peter, a real one and for you. I'm a process server, and earlier I knocked on your door hoping to give this to you. The lady who answered the door invited me in by mistake, but I couldn't resist. Perhaps God did send me."

"Maybe so. Anyway, I'll take care of the bill I owe. No problem. I'd forgotten about it really. But I'm glad you came."

"Peter, I'm glad too. Here's my card in case you'd like to talk sometime."

Driving back along Bridgeway, I could barely believe it had all happened. It was late. I'd been at Peter's over an hour. My plan had been to hit a couple serves in Santa Venetia on the way back, but it was too late. It had been a good night all in all.

Chapter 30

Good Night, Mr. Knight

J. Dallas Knight was supposed to be hard, if not impossible, to serve.

Our client had been trying to serve a notice of entry of judgment from another state for many months. Nevada was the state. The dollar amount of the judgment was significant, and the client had paid out a great deal of money to process servers and private investigators, but to no avail. Now it was our turn.

Terry took the call, and I could see he was giving the caller his tough guy approach.

"Why did you call us?"

"What makes you think we can do it when others have failed?"

"It's going to cost big bucks, and no guarantees."

Putting his hand over the mouthpiece, Terry swiveled his chair around so he could talk to me. "The defendant lives in a security building in the City. Nobody's been able to serve him. Good money. Wanna try?"

"Thirty an hour and thirty a mile?" I asked. Terry nodded yes.

"My partner says he'll do it," Terry said, as he turned back to the phone, "but it's thirty bucks an hour and thirty cents a mile." There was a considerable pause during which Terry played with his moustache, smoked his cigarette, and drank his coffee.

"Put it in the mail. We'll do our best on it."

J. Dallas Knight, a super evader, wary, tucked away, and nearly inaccessible—a good job at thirty and thirty.

In a few days, a fat letter arrived with two copies of the legal document, two typed pages of an account of previous attempts and pertinent details, plus a picture. A very big man, Knight looked to be in his fifties, bearded, unfriendly, potentially violent, addicted to young women and cocaine, liking the bars on Union Street, especially Perry's, would even hang out at the Bank Exchange in the Trans America Pyramid, and lived in an old-buy elegant apartment building at the Bay end of Hyde.

A notice of entry of judgment from a sister state is like a summons and complaint in that it is not dated. There is the usual response time, so I was under no time pressure. I studied the picture intensely so I would have no trouble identifying him.

On a Thursday night, I drove into the City for my first attempt. Sitting in the Tercel in front of my house, I noted the time and mileage. I'd even get the bridge fare back. Coming off the Golden Gate, I drove to Lombard, crossed Van Ness and Polk, and turned left on Hyde. The apartment building was on a corner. There was no place to park, and I ended up finding a space on Polk. The steep walk up from Polk to Hyde wasn't appreciated. I'd had too many cups of coffee, and the urge was heavily upon me. Walking uphill pushed the button, but the night-lights around the apartment intimidated me. I'd have to hold it.

As was typical of San Francisco's big apartments, there was no access to the individual units. Instead, there was a buzzer and an intercom. I already knew from the report on previous attempts that ringing Knight directly would be

30 – Good Night, Mr. Knight

doomed to failure. There were two other options. One, ring the manager and lie my way in. Or, two, push the buzzer of every apartment and hope someone would let me in. I went for the first. The manager, who sounded like an elderly woman, buzzed me in when I told her I had a delivery for Mr. Knight but that he wasn't home, so I needed to set it at his door. Great, I was in. There were four stories plus a basement. Knight lived in the basement. The building was old, with antique furniture scattered about the broad, dimly lit halls, and a Persian carpet, which seemed ancient and made my approach to Knight's door a quiet one.

With considerable anticipation, I knocked and knocked, listening with my ear to the door after each knock. The place seemed cold. I felt very letdown. Of course, if I'd gotten him so early, the bill to the client would have been small, with the only satisfaction being a job well done. With Knight absent, I would have to proceed to Perry's on Union, maybe the Bus Stop, maybe even 2001, and if Union Street failed me, I'd head downtown to the Bank Exchange, but probably not Barnaby's.

Walking back along the corridor in the tomb-like place, the urge hit me again. Down the hall from Knight's door, I saw a small wood table with a vase on it containing a flower. A terrible idea struck me. The excitement of the hunt had temporarily relieved me of the need, but now that it was back, and it was stronger than ever. My mind was made up when I saw that the flower placed in the clear glass vase was plastic. I lifted the flower out and turned the white glass vase into a yellow vase (I take a lot of vitamins). Setting the now warmed vase back down on the table, I put the flower in. I wondered how long it would be before anyone noticed.

It was early, about seven, when I arrived at Perry's. Parking was terrible; there was no place at the bar; I was smoking everyone else's cigarettes, and I was substantially underdressed in my tennis shoes, jeans (not designer), and an old red flannel shirt. Leaning against the fake bronze railing, I drank a beer. After the first swallow, I was certain J. Dallas Knight was not at Perry's. So, I looked at the ladies. Only one looked back, and there was no mistaking the look of disgust in her eyes.

The Bus Stop was much the same, except it was not as crowded. The ladies were not as dressed up, so I fit in better, but the guys were cowboy macho, and I was country dumb looking. After another beer, I walked down to 2001, walked up to the entrance, and decided against it. I didn't need to be given an all too quick once-over by a bunch of young Arab girls.

Before leaving Union Street all together, I walked down to DeLancey Street Restaurant, looked for Knight there, too, and had another beer. No Knight, no ladies either. In fact, no one was in the place but me. No Knight, but I was on the clock and making money.

Driving downtown seemed like a waste to me. However, I at least wanted to kill some time before making another attempt at Knight's apartment.

Parking was simple, a spot right in front of the Trans America Building, the side with the main entrance to the Bank Exchange. Although it was a weeknight, the place was crammed. I was a bit above the average age, but didn't feel out of place. It seemed like every race and nationality was present, a real human menagerie.

Standing against the bar, I ordered another beer and began to look around. Next to me was a young, beautiful black girl, dressed in white satin, who, it was clear, was wearing no underclothes. She gave me a once over; I grimaced back, trying to ignore her, which wasn't easy.

"I only drink Courvoisier. The best. I always go with class. That's me."

30 – Good Night, Mr. Knight

She was smashed and I guessed it had been a free drunk.

"Only the best for you, like that dress. I sure like the way you wear it."

"It's just the natural me. Do you like the natural me?"

"You're beautiful."

"I need another Courvoisier."

"You do?"

"See, empty again, honey. I drink natural."

"Well, I'm glad to hear that."

She grabbed a cocktail girl and ordered her drink. It was clear I'd get hit for it. I wasn't up to it.

"Hope you enjoy your drink. See you later."

"Hey, you can't leave now. You bastard – come back here."

Hoping to spot Knight, I walked along the edge of the dance floor to a far end of the place while the pretty black drunk was yelling at me. Her voice drowned out the music a time or two.

Places like the Bank Exchange never did much for me. It seemed like it was a forum for chaos and lying. I felt bad for Knight if this was a favorite of his, at his age anyway.

After running up another hour, I walked outside into the cool night air. Once again, I understood what the phrase, "a breath of fresh air" was all about. Driving back to Hyde Street, I worked on a new plan to get into the building. It wouldn't work to try the manager again. I'd have to go with pushing buttons until I was buzzed in.

Out of twelve apartments, I got only two responses and the line about losing my key didn't work. I faked drunkenness, slurring my speech, pleading to be let in, yet nothing worked. Try as I might, I couldn't come up with anything better.

Two weeks went by before I tried again, hoping any talk about someone trying to get into the building would die out. Knight was no doubt alert to attempts to serve him and I'd probably put him on guard.

Next time, I picked a Friday night. The manager had gotten me in before, so I thought I'd try it again. Much to my delight, I was buzzed in as soon as I pressed the bell. Once again, I was inside and the sense that I was going to get J. Dallas Knight was strong on me.

As I approached the central hall from which the major corridors ran off, I heard a voice above me.

"Are you Jim?" It was the manager, I guessed, three floors up looking at me down the stair well.

"Yes."

"We've been waiting for you. Mr. Knight just called and said he was having dinner but would be ready in half an hour. He wanted you to wait with me until then."

Jim Ross was my phony name, but this had to be a mistake. I'd go with it I thought, but not to the point of waiting in the manager's apartment. Another Jim would no doubt be along.

"You know, ma'am, I'll step down and see Knight for a moment, then I'll be up."

"Please come up, we have a lot to discuss. I'm very worried about this."

"Okay, I'll be right up." I hated to lie to her. She was so distressed, but the real Jim was probably coming up the walk.

Down the stairs, around the bend, past the plastic flower and vase, the water therein was clearer in color, but still slightly yellow, and up to the door of J. Dallas Knight. Before knocking, I listened at the door. Two people were inside, a man and a woman.

I knocked, medium hard, and waited. My heart was racing; the paper was in my hand. Heavy steps approached. "Who's there?"

"Jim." The door swung open.

"Who are you?"
"Jim Ross."
"So."
"I'm a process server, Mr. Knight. This is for you."

It was Knight, too; he looked just like his picture. A big, bearded man, quite distinguished looking. A massive scowl marred his handsome face.

"How'd you get in here?"

"I'm rather clever, and I had to be since, you're very evasive. But I got you, didn't I?"

He reached out calmly and took the paper from my hand. Instead of being angry, he was crestfallen and sad looking, as though he'd lost the big game all by himself. He said not another thing.

"Good night, Mr. Knight," I said, with a careful grin. I turned and headed back down the corridor, stopping only long enough to freshen the water in the flower vase, and then out into the night of San Francisco. Another breath of fresh air with the only decision before me being Perry's or the Bank Exchange.

Chapter 31

The View from #4

My weekday is broken up into four parts. Get the mail in the morning, serve businesses till noon or so, afternoon free for a couple hours, and out again around six. At first, I detested the schedule; now I appreciate it. Afternoons are wonderful for getting family errands accomplished, and then there is time for tennis, working out, writing, and napping. After it's all wrapped up, I like to sit a while in various bars and cafés and read the paper or converse with the locals. Now that I'm remarried, I get to do this a little less often. It's a great life.

And having a job is a good thing in '82-'83, any job, especially a good one like mine. Just this moment, I did some figuring and found I made very close to twenty thousand bucks as a process server in 1982. That's twice the best I ever did as a minister.

However, it's not all glitter and gold.

December of 1982 brought with it a few solid storms to Marin—high winds, considerable rain, normal winter weather. On the stormiest night of them all, I was in Sausalito up in the hills above Sally Stanford's place. I felt like my Tercel was going to be blown into the Bay. The water was high, seemingly about to swamp Bridgeway. White caps crowded one another on the blue-black surging mass of bay water: beautiful and powerful in the night.

The hour was late, but I had only one serve left, a summons and complaint for a guy on Bonita Street. I'd made a number of attempts over a two-week period and had had no luck. In each previous attempt, there had been no one home. It was not any kind of evasion; simply no one had been there. But the storm may have been working for me, because the place I wanted was flooded with yellow light. My heard leapt within me, almost in a spiritual way. Religion and process serving share some common ground.

That good old sense of satisfaction filled me as I climbed out of my car. The paper was tucked into my coat pocket; my glasses were left behind on the passenger seat, and I held my hat on my head as I splashed across the street.

I wanted a Jerome Bacca. The house was a quadraplex, one and two on the bottom, three and four on top. Bacca lived in four. It was an old wood structure, slightly modernized, but I could tell the place was dilapidated by the feel of the wood under my feet. The ledge or walkway in front of the upper level apartments was extraordinarily narrow, and the railing seemed all too flimsy. The rain made the worn planking slippery under my feet. I didn't' want any trouble up there.

The place shone bright with lights, and the door was slightly ajar. Taking the paper out of my pocket, I held it in my hand, ready to transfer it like a baton into the hands of the defendant or anyone else over eighteen who might be able to crawl to the door.

Once, twice, three times I knocked. Nothing. Curtains of thin strips of bamboo allowed me to see easily into the apartment. It looked like every light was on in every room. No sound from the TV, and I couldn't hear any music. I could see a desk and its lamp was on. I could see the bed; it was empty. I could even see into the bathroom. No one was on the toilet and a perfectly placed mirror allowed me to see into the shower stall. Empty.

With a good strong voice, I yelled "Jerome, Jerome." All was quiet. Someone had to be home or would be back momentarily. I decided to wait.

Fortunately, a short overhang kept most of the rain off me. The waiting was made bearable by a terrific fight that was staged directly across the street. From my vantage point, I had a perfect view of the whole thing. First, he stormed out the front door yelling back at her, whom I could see inside the house. He jumped into his car and gunned away. She went to the kitchen, picked up a pack of cigarettes from the kitchen table, picked one out and lit up. Then she opened the refrigerator door and took out a beer. For a few seconds, she tried twisting the cap off, gave up, found an opener in a cabinet, and opened her beer. The beer was to only serve as a chaser. From underneath a counter, she produced a liquor bottle. It looked like a fifth of Old Grand Dad. A little of that stuff goes a long way at 114 proof. Whatever it was, she tossed down a good gulp right out of the bottle. She held that short brown bottle straight up for a full two seconds. Putting it down, she gagged and covered her eyes and mouth with her hands. In a moment, she recovered and swigged out of the beer bottle, clearly a Coors. One swig, then another real short one. She stood there, still, for a good ten seconds, then she wheeled around and disappeared into the back part of the house. In a flash, she was back, coat on, purse in hand, a very pretty woman in her late twenties. I was just thinking of going over to comfort her, but she was out the door, headed to a car parked right in front of mine. There was some delay at the car door. Finally, she placed her purse on the top of the car and went through it thoroughly. That worked, so soon she too gunned it down the street.

Having run out of entertainment, I went back on the job. Using a quarter, I rapped sharply on the door and called out "Jerry, Jerry." I was feeling a little desperate. Just as I was about to leave, a car screeched to a halt in front of the house across the street. It was the guy in the fight. He was back. He ran up the steps and into the house. I could hear him shouting out for the lady. After a couple of minutes, he discovered the whiskey and the beer in the kitchen. With a hand on each, he stood figuring it out. He nodded and seemed to smile to himself, and then he tipped both bottles up, the strong stuff first, then the one, two again. He was about to take a third double whammy when the lady screeched up to the house. She parked the car nearly in the center of the street, banged the car door shut and ran up into the house. They met in the front hallway, embraced, hugged, and headed into the dark recesses of the house. All was well.

However, I was yet in the rain with a legal paper in my hand and no one to serve it to.

At the very last moment before my departure, I looked into the apartment again. And there, standing right in the living room was a bearded man in his mid-thirties. It was like a magical appearance. Mine was not to reason why. I knocked, and the door opened.

"Hi. Jerome?"

"Oh, no, Jerome lives right next door in number three."

"Oh, really?"

"Right." And he shut the door.

Either he was awfully slick, or I was awfully stupid. There I was, standing in the dark with my paper. It had all happened so fast.

Okay, I went to number three. Within a few seconds of my knock, the door opened, a face said, "Yes," and I said,

"Jerome?" and the face said, "No, he lives in number four." And he shut the door. Again, it had all happened so fast.

As I reflect back, I believe I was somewhat numbed by the cold. But I was thinking well enough to know I could check the mailboxes. At the foot of the stairs, on the street level, were four mailboxes, and on each one was a number and a name. Very simple. On number four, printed on a piece of white tape was the name, "Jerome Bacca." The tape was rather new, too, not more than a month old. Whoever was at apartment four, Bacca or not, was going to get a legal document.

As determined as the night would allow, I renegotiated the rickety way back up the stairs. Before knocking, I looked into the window of number four. My man was visible, walking back and forth in the tiny kitchen. I watched him as I rapped on the wood frame of the door. He looked at the door with an irritated expression on his face, then walked rapidly to it and me

"Jerome Bacca lives here. And you are Jerome Bacca. Right?"

"I told you he lives next door."

"That's not what the mailbox says. Come on, I know Bacca lives here."

He was becoming visibly upset. I could have merely thrown the paper down and counted it as a subserve, but I was enjoying the cat and mouse game.

"Look, Bacca isn't here."

"He lives here then? Well, I'll tell you the truth. I have a legal paper for him, a summons and complaint. Actually, he's being sued for a fairly hefty amount. And I'm going to leave it with you, whoever you are. And it doesn't matter. Bacca lives here, and you live here, so I'm going with a subserve. Bacca has forty, rather than, thirty days to respond." I held out the paper. He refused to take it, so I let it flutter to the floor inside the apartment.

31 – The View from #4

He was nearing the point of rage. His body language told me he would have liked to have charged me and punched me out. I moved to the side of the door and near the side of the house. The flimsy railing I knew was only two feet in back of me. The footing was precarious, and any fight could have been highly dangerous. As was my custom in the face of fisticuffs, I held my hands up level with my shoulders, palms open, at once a ready position and conciliatory gesture.

"Leave right now or I'll call the police," he said, barely holding himself in check.

I smiled. "Oh, please do. I'll wait right here. For sure I'll find out who you are." And I stood there smiling.

With a classic soccer style swing of the leg, he kicked the paper out of the door and over the railing. A wind caught it and carried it out onto the street. Still smiling and with my hands up, I watched the paper tumble and spin in the wind as it floated off into the darkness.

"Nice kick , buddy." Poor Bacca though. In forty days, he'll probably be in default, then there will be liens, attachments, garnishments, repossessions, and who knows what else.

"Bacca wasn't served. The paper is gone."

"Sure, now it is. Do you know what it would cost Bacca to challenge the service of process? And he'd lose. I'm beginning to think you're not too bright. Do you think it works to throw traffic tickets away? Anyway, I'm going, unless you're going to call the police, in which case I'll wait. And I'd put my hat and coat on if I were you and retrieve that paper. Bacca is certainly going to want it."

One last time, I negotiated the slippery stairs. I drove down Bonita one block, crossed Caledonia, and stopped at Bridgeway. There on the corner, one of Sausalito's street people was holding the legal paper that had been booted onto Bonita. I doubt if it made very interesting reading.

Chapter 32

Motorboat to the Door

"This will be a tough one. Are you willing to do a very out of the ordinary serve?"

I kicked back in my chair, put my boots up on the desk. "Tell me about it," I said, as I cradled the phone receiver on my shoulder.

The person on the other end was an attorney in Los Angeles. His client owned a houseboat in Sausalito, a big one, worth a quarter of a million or so. And the owner had made the mistake of renting it out to an unknown character who had refused to pay the $1,400 rent for a number of months. Now, it was time for a Three-Day Notice to Pay Rent or Quit to be served.

"There won't be any problem with the notice," I replied, "That can be posted."

"I'd like personal service, but a posting would be okay."

"What kind of problems are you anticipating?"

"Well, this guy has a retractable walkway and if it's up, like a drawbridge, you can't get to the door. The sheriff can't even serve him. Another process serving firm has tried to do it, but nothing so far."

"You've been through this before then?"

"In the past, the mailing of a thirty-day notice brought

results, but it's been months this time. I've called, but the number is disconnected. We don't think he works, but he is a card player, and he entertains people almost every weekend from Friday right to Sunday night. He puts on some pretty wild events. And, I want to be careful to say this, we understand he can be violent."

"Violent. Well, that always costs more. What do you have in mind?"

"How about a double fee?"

"Forty, then."

"Forty."

"Mail me the notice and we'll see how it is."

Two days later on a Thursday, a Three-Day Notice for Jamie Sutter of Kappas Marina, Sausalito, arrived. The attorney sent only one copy, so I had to make another. I wasn't terribly impressed with that little failure. While I made out he worksheet, I discussed the matter with my partner, Terry.

"How do you think I ought to handle it?"

Terry thought for a moment. "Try it this afternoon, get a feel for the place, and if you have no luck, try Friday evening before dark."

"What if the walkway is up? It seems like posting the notice on the dock itself in front of the houseboat would do it."

"It would be questionable. Better go for a personal serve or tacking it onto the door. Give it a shot and see what happens."

That Thursday afternoon, in mid-Spring, I rolled into Kappas Marina on Gate 6 Road. Sutter's place wasn't hard to spot. It was the biggest and fanciest houseboat around, ornate, three-storied, made of wood, with angles to boggle the mind. Its real stain-glass windows made quite an impression. And the walkway was up, with the Bay itself acting as a moat. The tide was out, and the muscles and barnacles clung by the thousands to the foundation of the houseboat. The stink of decaying sea things mingled with other waste producing a rather sharp odor.

The walkway itself was a piece of art. I could see the machinery used to construct it, and it was substantial. There was simply no way to get up to the door.

It didn't look like anyone was home. No lights shone, no music was playing, and no brightening and darkening of light, the tell-tale sign of a television going, was evident. Walking down thirty or so yards from the houseboat, I leaned against the dock railing for a few minutes, meditating on the job. There were only two ways to get to the houseboat. One was by the walkway. The other was by boat. I could see a large deck on the back with various kinds of outdoor furniture scattered about. No doubt, there was a back door, probably a sliding glass door, but a door at any rate. Of course, I had no boat, yet that would be a possibility. A risky possibility.

Friday evening I was back about seven-thirty. There was still a little light in the sky, not much, but the lights from the houseboats provided plenty of illumination. Stutter's houseboat was well-lit. I could see people's shadows passing back and forth behind the stain-glass windows. There was no mistaking Fleetwood Mac on the stereo. The houseboat had a festive look to it. My job was to spoil the fun.

The walkway was down. My only hope was to catch someone arriving and get up to the door by almost forcing my way. As I considered the possible consequences of such a maneuver, I began feeling weakish and slightly less confidant. If Sutter had a phone, I'd have even called and asked him to cooperate. Desperate now, I thought about yelling out to him from the dock. As I was in the midst of my second-guessing, a very gorgeous woman stopped beside me. She gave me a pleasant hello.

"Have you rung Jamie?" she asked.
"No, I just got here myself."
"Well, are you going to do that?"
"This is my first time here."
"You don't know where the buzzer is, do you? Here it is, in this little drawer."

She reached down, opened a little wooden compartment built into the railing and pressed a white colored buzzer. In a moment, the front door of the houseboat swung open, and a man looked out.

"Sherry. Hey, you look beautiful."
"Jamie, how are you?"
"Sherry, who's that you're with?"
"Oh, nobody, he was here when I got here."
"How you doing," he sent in my direction, "who are you?"
"I'm Jim Ross. I need to see you for a minute."
"Okay, come on down."

Normally I would have been highly excited in the face of such a grand success. But I wasn't too thrilled for some reason.

The drawbridge slowly descended and locked in place. Sherry stepped up and started down. I followed.

Sherry was ushered in; I stuttered around on the narrow front deck. Sutter gave me a once-over. He was about forty, athletic type, big, and he had a worldly-wise look to him.

"What'd you say your name was?"
"Jim Ross."
"What can I do for you?"
"I have a paper for you." I pulled it out of my pocket, unfolded it, and handed it to him.
"Well, you son-of-a-bitch." Without moving, he reached for and pressed the button that controlled the drawbridge. It lifted off the dock before I realized what had happened.

Now I was stranded.

"Hey, everybody," he shouted into the house, "We've got a damn process server out here who is trying to evict us."

It sounded like a stampede as people hurried to the front door. Backing against the wall, I tried to look calm. My idea was to keep quiet, offer no offense and hope to smile my way out. Immediately, the idea, "False imprisonment" struck me, but I thought I'd hold that threat in reserve. Looking at the oozy muck the Bay had for a bottom in that part of Sausalito, I was sure I'd sink up to my eyeballs if I attempted to jump for it.

"Mr. Sutter, I'm a process server; your landlords' attorney is my client. I have nothing to do with anything." I was speaking to a dozen people at least.

"Shut your mouth, creep. You lied your way into here."

"No, while I was on the dock, you invited me down."

"You should have told me right away who you were. You tricked me, you jerk."

"Look, I've got a job to do, and I did it. Now, I have to leave."

"You can leave anytime, man, anytime."

"Okay, lower the drawbridge then, please."

"Screw you, jerk."

It had come down to it. I had one more chance.

"Mr. Sutter, you have me imprisoned here. I have no safe way out. Your own act has done this, and you refuse to let me go. Maybe one of your friends here is a lawyer and will tell you of the jam you could be in if I were to press it."

Sutter thought about it; he was still in control of himself. Actually, I was glad there was a crowd on hand to witness it all. By himself, I was sure there would have been a fight.

"So, call a cop."

"Sutter, you really want a fight, don't you? Well, I'll give it to you, and you'll have a battery charge against you. Not too long from now, one way or another, you're going to be in jail." With that, I turned sideways preparing to hit him.

"All right, all right, get your ass off here and never come back or I'll shoot your ass." He pressed the button, and the drawbridge began to stretch out to the dock. Knowing he had to maintain face, I said nothing as I waited for my avenue to safety descend.

Without another word, I walked the space between houseboat and dock and hurried away. The observers, Sutter's friends, merely watched; not a one said a word. Sutter was obviously the dominant personality.

Sitting in my car in the parking lot, making out my worksheet, I had a sick felling, a kind of emotional shaking. That situation, I knew, could have been disastrous. I will fight, but I don't want to. Fights produce all kinds of trouble, and it doesn't take much for something irreversibly terrible to happen. Usually after a tough serve, I have that exhilarating sense of success that keeps me going, but not this time. Hopefully, Sutter would pay his rent so I wouldn't be asked to serve an unlawful detainer on him.

By Monday, the experience with Sutter was little more than an unpleasant memory. Terry wasn't amused as I related the houseboat serve.

"You barley made it out of that one. I don't know what we'll do if we get a U.D. for him. If we do, and we probably will, we'll get diligence and post it some way. Anyway, I'm going to call the attorney and let him know what happened. I wonder if they'll throw in a tip. They might. They really wanted this one."

An unlawful detainer for Sutter was in Friday morning's mail. Neither Terry nor I were pleased. But a job is a job. Over the weekend, I got diligence. I went there Friday night, drawbridge up, protecting his party again, lied about going there Saturday and Sunday to get in my three attempts, and Monday morning told Terry to ask the attorney for a posting order. I had an idea.

By that next Thursday, the posting order had been signed by a municipal court judge and had been filed with the Superior court. Now for the idea. My plan was to take a boat out to the houseboat, climb onto the back deck and tape the legal paper to the back door. It was going to cost though.

"Terry, let's hit the attorney up for a good amount on this. We're going to have to find a boat, I'd say at least a hundred, maybe a hundred and a half plus expenses."

"Well, it can't be too much, not a hundred, maybe fifty, plus expenses."

"No way, I'm not doing it alone. You're going to be in that boat with me."

"Right, at least a hundred, plus expenses."

"And if the attorney won't go for it, forget it."

The attorney did go for it, and he settled for a hundred and a quarter plus expenses, the expenses being the boat.

Terry and I finally agreed to Saturday afternoon for our cruise on the Bay. We met at Gate Five Road and Bridgeway near where the hookers stand to hitch rides for twenty bucks or so.

"First, we need a boat," I said. "My guess is a motorboat would do. Let's try down by Jerry's Marina."

Jerry's Marina, the dock, and the bait store were alive with people, but it wasn't what we needed. Next, we went to Anderson's Boat Yard at the Clipper Yacht Harbor. Lines and lines of sloops, yawls, and ketches sat in their berths. We walked into Anderson's where a bunch of guys were working on boats that sat on mammoth slings held up by cranes.

"My friend and I need to rent a motorboat for half an hour."

All we got was a few funny looks.

32 – Motorboat to the Door

As we were pulling out of Anderson's, one of the workmen walked out a ways towards us and yelled, "Wait a minute."

Terry backed up, changed directions and headed into Sanderson's.

The guy who had hailed us came up to Terry's window. "What do you need?"

"A motorboat, half an hour, at say, $20 an hour." Terry replied.

"Twenty bucks? No, forty bucks, okay."

"You got it. But we need to do it now."

"You got it. Park over there and let's go. Let me see the forty."

We weren't prepared for that. I didn't have so much as five.

"Terry, I'm basically broke. I hope you've got it."

"Would you take a check?" Terry asked.

"No, sorry, but I need to see the forty, have it in my hand before I start it up."

My partner was not very happy about it, because he did have the money.

"Look, Terry, you'll get it back Monday. It's all covered, right? Come on; let's get on with it. Remember, 'It goes with territory.'"

"Shit."

The boat had four seats. I sat in the stern by myself: me and the legal paper. Terry was along, but I was going to do the dirty work.

We shot north along the Bay. It was not long till we rounded the mass of houseboats jutting out of Kappas Marina. Terry was acting as pilot, pointing out the particular destination. He never informed the owner of the boat what was up. Sitting alone in the stern of the boat, I felt what might be described as dread. I leaned forward and told Terry to have the engine cut so we could glide up to

Sutter's houseboat without any noise.

It was really a nice day, no swells, no white caps, no breeze— unusual. Perfect day. The motorboat slid through the water so silently when the engine was cut.

The sun shone at such an angle that I couldn't see into the windows at the rear of Sutter's houseboat. There was, of course, a door, double French doors, the top half, stained glass. The door, I was determined, would soon be adorned with a summons and complaint.

After parallel parking alongside the houseboat, I grabbed the top of the rail that enclosed the deck, stood up, and climbed over it. It felt as though a hundred eyes inside Sutter's were watching me. Without being quiet, or careful, I walked quickly to the door, and with one thumb tack, stuck the paper to the side of the door, turned, and walked just as quickly back to the rail and the boat. Once in, I couldn't help it.

"Sutter. Sutter. Hey, Sutter," I yelled out.

In a moment, he was out on the deck, he and a few others.

"Sutter, a present for you just behind you. That's an unlawful detainer. It means eviction, Sutter. So long."

The skipper of the motorboat gunned the engine to life and speed away. And he was not happy. When we got back to Anderson's, he told us he was a friend of Sutter's. Terry and I endured a tongue-lashing, a challenge to a fight, and other indignities as we walked to Terry's car.

"A hundred and twenty-five dollars," Terry said.

"Plus forty, Terry."

Chapter 33

Being Blind

January of 1983 was extremely slow, not much to serve, so of course there were small paychecks. The third Thursday in January, I rolled into the office with only one serve to turn in. I signed the proof of service, kicked back in my chair and complained about the lack of work.

"Terry, we could use some business. I wish we could manufacture some ourselves. Instead, we have to wait for the mail and the phone."

"One or two slow days and you're worried. Relax, things will pick up again. In fact, something did come in. I'm not going to do it, but you can if you want."

"What came in?" Almost anything would be better than my boredom.

"An old friend of mine called, a lawyer I've done some detective work for. Not much money, but real detective stuff, and I'm not going to do it. I told him I'd offer it to you though."

"Okay, I'll give it a try."

"You want to do it, and you don't even know what it is?"

"Okay, okay, tell me what it is."

"A blind man got cheated and short-changed at a lunch shack in the City. You'd have to disguise yourself as a blind man and see if it happened again. If it does, a criminal action as well as a big lawsuit could come out of it. That could mean court appearances, maybe over a long period, who knows."

"How come there's no money?"

"My lawyer friend operates out of a tiny office, no secretary, the bare minimum, so he hasn't any money in back of him. The blind guy has nothing."

"How much money?"

"Thirty bucks plus expenses, and the expenses have to be minimal."

"What kind of expenses?"

"Oh, bus fare—you've got to arrive by bus. The money you're going to use to buy something, at least a twenty, but the white cane and dark glasses will be furnished. That's it."

"I'm going to make half of thirty bucks. What else do you know about it?"

"You heard it all. There is no more."

"Tell the guy I'll do it. If someone is cheating a blind man , at least I can do something righteous for a change."

A week went by and there was nothing else on the case. Finally, I had Terry call his lawyer friend to find out about it. The more I thought of the blind man and the lunch shack, the more I wanted to get on with it, even though the money was bad. I even tried faking blindness and found I'm glad I'm not blind. My work took me into the City, and while there, I checked the lunch shack out. There was a bus stop directly in front of the tiny establishment, which served soda pop, hot dogs, coffee and the like from a walk-up window. One lone Asian of some type manned the place. I watched the goings on for ten minutes or so, and even though it was early afternoon, only one woman stopped for a coke. The business was a sad looking place with dirty windows, old signs, and high prices. The one thing it had going for it was a good location. No doubt hundreds of people passed it every quarter hour. The job would be easy when it came time to do it.

The second week of February was half gone before the blind man's attorney called to say the white cane and dark glasses were ready. I was glad to get on with it, since I'd told a few people about the job, and I think some of them wondered about me, as I always had to answer their inquiries with "not yet."

The white cane was made of metal and was jointed with a bungee type cord through the center. It could be disjointed and folded into a small package. Overall, it was nearly five feet in length and had a red tip. It was nearly impossible for someone to see my eyes through the sturdy horned-rim dark glasses. When I put on an "old man's" hat, the kind my dad wore when he sold Fuller Brushes in Portland, Oregon, during the late forties and early fifties, and wore my long blue Air Force raincoat, I looked like a fifty year old blind man.

Being blind, I found, presented many problems. It was easy to realize the great difficulty a blind person faced. It is a different world all together. In high school, I'd gone with a friend to dances at a school for the blind in San Fernando Valley. In fact, the first girl I ever really kissed was blind. At one of the dances, one girl I was dancing with said, "I'm sweet sixteen and never been kissed." I was fourteen at the time. I said, "Me, too" and hurriedly walked away, leaving the girl puckered and waiting. Sitting down outside against a wall, I trembled a while. After going through a myriad of emotions, it came to me how hurt the girl must have been. Several dances had elapsed by that time. Re-entering, I looked for her but couldn't find her. I found my friend and explained the situation. He looked all over for her, too, and eventually, we realized she was not on the dance floor or anywhere in the gym.

Toward the end of the dance, I wandered outside and found her sitting on a wooden bench beside a drinking fountain She was kind of cute; of course, her eyes blinked and moved in unusual ways. At fourteen, I didn't know how to kiss a girl, but I did my best. And my best was good enough. We smooched more than a few times and would have gone on indefinitely had my friend not found us. That was the end of it; I don't recall going to any more of the dances. There was a beach party, but the first girl I'd ever kissed wasn't there.

There is not much actor in me, and I knew I didn't have to carry the masquerade too far, so it was more for fun and experience than anything else, and I practiced being blind. However, I couldn't do it without opening my eyes. After a few seconds of knocking about with the cane, I'd feel uneasy about something and cheat.

On a rainy Tuesday morning in February, I headed out for the City. The bus stopped every two blocks along the busy downtown street. Finding a parking space one block above the snack shack, I walked on the opposite side of the street to the bus stop four blocks below the place. My hat was on my head, but the cane and the dark glasses, I kept in the pocket of my raincoat. Directly in back of the bus stop was an old time San Francisco office building. It didn't matter much if anyone saw me putting on the glasses and pulling out the cane, yet I wanted to do it unobserved. Not finding any hiding place in the lobby, I took the elevator to the second floor, found a bathroom and walked out of the building a few minutes later as a blind man.

We treat the blind differently. Most everyone walked way around me and very few really looked at me. It was quite unusual. I could see the people around me, but they didn't know it. At first, I made eye contact, out of habit, and I wondered if people knew I could see. After a few minutes, I learned to look above, below, or to the side of a person's head and in doing so, I noticed I inclined my head slightly to one side or the other.

Waiting for the bus, I sat on a wooden bench with my hands folded on my lap, holding the cane out in front of me, the cane tip extending an inch or two over the edge of the curb. My raincoat fit me when I received it at age nineteen in the military, but now it was too small, and the sleeves needed three or four more inches. My watch sparkled on my left wrist and as I focused on it, I felt I should not have it on. "What is a blind man doing with a watch?" Terry later told me the blind have watches with faces that lift back with raised dots on the face. But I didn't know that, so I took the watch off and slipped it into my coat pocket.

Must have been that I'd just missed a bus, because it seemed like I sat waiting for a long time. It was a rare quiet time for me. I'm probably a workaholic; at least, I'm "Always on the go," as my mother used to say. Doing my job as a blind man, I had to sit and be calm. I could feel my body settling down from the customary tense state. Thinking was unrushed and pleasant. A bus came and I merely sat there. The driver asked me if I wanted on and I said no. I wanted to be peaceful some more.

By the time the next bus pulled up, though, I was ready to go. It flashed through my mind that I'd find a ticket on my windshield if I didn't get on with it.

Bus drivers, at least the two I dealt with, were very kind and helpful. The driver of the bus I boarded waited patiently as I fumbled with my change, and he directed me to a seat. Tapping around with the cane, I finally slumped into a seat. The bus didn't move until I was seated.

I was pleasantly surprised.

In a few minutes, I was making my way down the stairs of the bus with the dismal little snack shack directly in front of me. There was a customer at the window at the time of my arrival, making me feel that I was not being watched by the counter person. By the time I reached the place, the customer was gone. Rather than coming perfectly to the window, I missed it by two feet.

"Do you have hot dogs?"

"Yes. Large or small?"

"Oh, small please, with everything."

"Okay, anything to drink?"

"Uh, do you have any hot chocolate?"

"Yes. Large or small?"

"Oh, small, I think. And could you make it so I could take it away?"

"That's the way we do it here, sir."

"Fine, fine."

I watched the preparations. A big fat hot dog it was. I was glad I had asked for a small, and it was Carnation instant with hot water. The bun was much smaller than the hot dog, a little dab of mustard was all I got and maybe a dozen little pieces of onions were sprinkled on. If I had not been feigning blindness, I would have complained.

"That'll be $1.83."

"Okay, here's a five," I said as I held out a ten.

"This is a ten you gave me."

"Oh, okay. I'm sorry."

She gave me the right change, placed a bag with the hot dog in it into my hand, set the Styrofoam cup, with plastic lid, down in front of me and turned away. That was it.

I had change in my hand, the cane, the bag and the cup. I'm clumsy anyway and I didn't do it right. The cup went first with a sploosh. The cane clattered to the sidewalk, second, followed closely by the change. I retained the bag.

Never have I had such a red face, burning hot. Off came the glasses. I bent over and picked up the cane, unjointed it and put it in my pocket and began chasing my money down. It was just terrible.

Naturally, I'd attracted a bit of a crowd. There was no way to clean it up and no one to be mad at. As best I could, I pulled my little scene together, grabbed my hot dog and walked up the street to my car. From forty yards away, I could see the red flag with the word "Expired" showing on the meter. If there had been a parking ticket waiting for me, I would have been extremely upset.

Chapter 34

Not a Dull Life

The rain of 1982/1983 was hard on me, especially during the months when it was dark so early. Cold hands, fogged windows, wet everything, up the side of a hill hunting for an address, narrow lanes I couldn't turn around in, people thinking I was crazy, people being hostile, dogs barking, slippery green slimy brick walkways, locked gates, nobody home, vacant houses—woe is me. But the money has been good, just enough to get by and keep the Tercel in tires and brakes. Twenty-eight thousand and some odd business miles in 1982. With no backup money in the bank, each month is crucial, every serve meaningful, every skip a loss.

Process serving is full of the unusual. The house with the "For Sale" sign, the lock box and the dark empty room, is the one you want. The only dark house on the street is the one you pull up in front of. Cars lining the street, the only place to park is in front of the address on the worksheet.

"Gee, that's funny, she moved out yesterday."

"You're looking for the Smiths, well, they sold us this house six years ago."

"My husband lives in L.A.; we're divorced."
"My daddy doesn't live here anymore."
"I'm afraid my father died last week."
"If you find him, let me know, will you? Here's my phone number. I have some serious business to discuss with that dead beat."
"He left five minutes ago."
"You can find him in the county jail."
"What are you? Some kind of bill collector?"
"I'm who you're looking for, asshole."
Few people say thank you, but some do.
"I don't know if I should say thank you," is an oft-heard response.

In most instances, I say, "So long" and there is only the sound of a door closing. That's the way I like it.

Some people lie to you. "You're looking for John Doe, sorry, he moved." I like to be lied to. At least I have a challenge.

"Well, I have the name, this very address. Therefore, I'm going to serve it. If, however, you can prove you are not John Doe, I'll take the paper with me." Occasionally, I hear a "Thank you" after such a serve.

Even more of a challenge is the guy who tells me he's going to throw me off his porch if I dare to leave a paper.

I've learned a few good lines.

"I know how you feel. I've been served several times myself."

Or, "If I don't serve it, my client will make be come back. Plus, I might even lose business, and I have to pay the rent. So, I hope you'll understand."

Or, "I don't want any trouble. My hand has just healed from the last fight."

Or, "Bruno wouldn't like that."

"Who's Bruno?"

"My friend who is out in the car waiting for me. You don't want to meet Bruno."

Or, "Okay, see you later." Then, when he shuts the door, I place the paper between the doorknob and the side of the door. A good serve.

Occasionally, I'll be made aware of the urgency of serving papers. Somebody always has something at stake, and from time to time, a great deal. And the lawyers fret, their clients fret, they want action, they are anxious, and they put the pressure on. Some people are desperately concerned that a person be served. And when I know that, I do my very best to take care of it. Regardless of how tough the serve was, generally only the attorney gets the thanks; the process server, almost never.

Perhaps there could be a 'Be kind to process servers' week. People will say, "How can you do such a terrible job? Why don't you get out of it?"

The thrill of making a good serve keeps me coming back. Strolling along Bridgeway in Sausalito with a summons and complaint in my pocket on a warm Tuesday afternoon is not a bad thing altogether. Touring the green hills of Fairfax or Mill Valley is enjoyable. I especially like Walden Lane in the Spring. Trips to the City can be especially rewarding. Pier 39, downtown, the financial district, even the Mission, China Basin, Union Street—great places, great views, strange people, good money, interesting stories to tell people. It's not a dull life.

Chapter 35

Is Serving for Misfits?

One reason process servers have such a bad reputation is that they are often misfits. Maybe "most often" is more descriptive. Process serving is an out-of-the-ordinary job, one that offers odd hours and the chance to be a fourth-rate detective. And there are few qualifications required, but a car is one of them, which eliminates a host of misfits who would like to try it. Desperation is a requirement. Many people say stupidity is, others suggest boldness. I think endurance has got to be high on the list. The pay is minimal, and especially at first, hard to come by. There is a grand illusion surrounding the job, unearned, but it keeps the misfits applying.

Owners of process serving businesses are often forced to hire people whom a war-time army would reject out-of-hand. But papers to serve pile up, clients are calling, hearing dates close, the office rent is due again, and the phone bill has got to be paid.

Jackie, the lady who taught me process serving and owns Marin Process Service, hired a guy out of sheer desperation, gave him a dozen papers to serve and had him utterly disappear. Not a call, not any contact from him for weeks. The calls from lawyers began coming in, excuses and apologies given, and the process server was nowhere to be found. Jackie had to play investigator in order to get the papers back. She located him in a cheap motel. She knocked and knocked. Finally, a voice answered, "Who is it?"

"It's Jackie. Do you have my papers?"

"Not now. I'll be in tomorrow."

"No, please. I need them now."

"Go away, would ya?"

Jackie turned the doorknob and found it was unlocked. Opening the door, she walked in, found the papers stuffed in a paper bag and made a quick exit. At least, she got the papers back, which is not always the case.

Chapter 36

Don't Assault a Process Server

Sacramento gave us some help, Kent. There's a new law that goes into effect January 1, 1984, that says anyone who assaults a process server gets one year in the county jail and a thousand dollar fine."

"Oh, is that right? I'd like to have the law printed on little cards we could hand out. If people knew about the new law, it could really help us."

Heading out to begin a stake-out in Sausalito early one Monday morning, I thought about the new law. It had been a long time since anyone had gotten tough with me. It seemed the longer I was on the job, the less trouble came my way. Not only don't I run into fights or near fights, but very few women have been throwing themselves at me lately. Perhaps, these two seemingly unrelated phenomena are tied together. Perhaps it has to do with my demeanor at the door; guys perceive me as macho and threatening while girls are not attracted to my suave masculine manner. I t might be wishful thinking, but It's too much for me to figure out.

A woman had given a bum check to a real estate agency for a piece of property. The complaint did not make a great deal of sense to me, because I had not gotten as far as the course in property while I attended San Francisco Law School. Somehow, the woman had been able to retain the property, or the money had been spent and was not recoverable or something. Anyhow, there was a plaintiff who wanted the check made good. Problem was the would-be defendant was a super evader. The cover letter from the attorney described her as mean, deceptive, and highly uncooperative. For a week, I had tried to make the serve the standard way and had failed on every attempt. Late Friday afternoon, I phoned the plaintiff's attorney and confessed that I had been unable to serve the paper and suggested a stakeout would get the job done. The attorney simply told me to get the paper served any way I could and not to worry about the cost. Words I love to hear.

A neighbor of the woman I wanted to serve had earlier eagerly pointed out to me the car and location of the back door of the defendant. It looked simple enough – be at the right spot by the car, wait for her to go to work, and surprise her with the summons and complaint. I had also found out that she was married, and the husband was a little wimp of a guy. The fact that they both went off to work together did not bother me.

By 6:20, January 30, I was at my post with the paper in my back pocket. I'd parked the Tercel out of view, since I was sure the woman had a fix on it. For an hour and a half, I sat beside a tree in some ivy, reading, first the Chronicle, then my Bible, then my Spanish lesson. The ground was hard and cold. Joggers gave me funny looks as they went by. Two dogs came up and sniffed me. An older gentleman, walking one of the dogs that sniffed me, stopped to talk a while. No doubt, the conversation might give me away and I put that untimely visit as the reason for my long wait. The neighbor had told me that the couple went to work between 6:30 and 7:00 without fail. The visit had occurred at 6:40. However, I was making a buck or two.

Happily, it was a pleasant day, even warm, and I was pleased to be where I was and to be doing what I was. Whenever I am in Sausalito at breakfast time and have a few dollars in my pocket that I can fritter away, I love to stop by Fred's for the feast they always put out. It was the thought of food that propelled me into action. At nine, I was due to give testimony in court and, if I was able to get to Fred's, I either had to leave or try and force the serve.

A good process server never gives up without a fight, so I decided to take a bold approach. Walking up the path in the back of the apartment, I climbed the steps to the back door. Just as I was about to knock, I glanced through a window into a bedroom. There on the bed was the couple, obviously frolicking under the covers. That made no difference to me. My sharp rapping on the window brought them up short. What glares they gave me!

"Joann Skarda, how are you doing? Sorry about this, but I have a legal paper for you. Of course, you know that, because you've been dodging me all week. But, here it is."

They neither one moved nor made a sound.

"Joann, look, I've got to give you this paper." With that, I held the paper up for her to see. Actually, I didn't know if this was going to be a good serve or not. I wished I hadn't gotten myself into such a mess. It dawned on me that I could get into one huge lawsuit. But what was done was done and I was determined to go through with it.

Still holding up the paper, I read the case title, loudly so I could be heard through the window.

Finally, I got some action.

"How dare you. You despicable beast. You give that to my lawyer," said Joann.

"Sorry, I can't. I have to give it to you."

"Well, I'm not getting up. You just leave that paper by the door and get out of here."

"You got it." And I did scoot as fast as I could.

Almost to my car, I heard a commotion behind me. Here was the husband running after me, dressed in a bathrobe and tennis shoes. My first impulse was to try and make a quick getaway, but I knew he would overtake me at the pace he was traveling. Slipping my watch off and laying my glasses on a nearby fence post, I turned to face the understandably outraged man. He was an ordinary-sized person, younger than me, a kind of unknown entity. He stopped five yards short of me and cinched up the tie cord to his bathrobe.

"All right, I'm really pissed off. And I'll tell you something right now, you're in big trouble."

This statement came in between puffings and shakings. I did not want any fight.

"You know, I am sorry about it. But it really was an accident. There you were. It just happened."

"There's no excuse. Now I'm going to use my martial arts on you."

"Gee, I hope you don't do that, but if you try, you're going to go to jail for one year and pay a thousand dollar fine. Do you think it's going to be worth it?"

"You are nothing but a process server."

"Well, okay, why don't you get with the fighting?"

It was just as well that I never found out about the martial arts or had to test the new law. At the right moment, the wife yelled down for him to come home that very second. He looked at me, turned to look toward where the shout came from, and decided to obey the voice.

Making out the worksheet in the car, I realized I still had time to eat at Fred's and make it back to the courthouse. Fred's was packed, of course, and I took the only seat in the place, a stool at the counter directly across from the orange juice squeezer. In the course of my meal, Fred came over to the squeezer and put a few oranges through it.

"Fred, yours is still the best there is."

Tall, friendly, hardworking, Fred said, "Thank you, thank you," as he concentrated on the oranges.

"Fred, I hope you don't mind but I mentioned your place here in my book. And all good stuff, too."

"Oh, good, good. Let me see a copy when it's ready."

"It'd be my pleasure."

Chapter 37

Ordinary Life Exposed

Sitting in the blue chairs in courtroom 9 at the Marin Civic Center, waiting for my arraignment, April 12, 1983, was not pleasant. I was there on a criminal charge—thank God, a misdemeanor. The letter from the office of the District Attorney read:

YOU HAVE BEEN CHARGED WITH A VIOLATION OF SECTION 602(1) of the Penal Code.

As if that were not enough, another paragraph read:

LEGAL APPEARANCE MUST BE MADE OR WE SHALL REQUEST THE COURT TO ORDER A WARRANT FOR YOUR ARREST.

It was signed by Susan Stanfield-Elias, deputy district attorney.

The notice said I was to be in court at 9:30 AM. I was there at 9:15, wearing a white shirt and tie with coat: none of which helped the anxiety I felt.

Promptly at 9:30 AM, the bailiff called the court to order

and announced the arrival of Judge Stephens.

Judge Stephens is a municipal court judge, and I'd seen him many times. On probably a dozen occasions, he'd signed various court orders for me. He is black, about forty-five, polite, deliberate, considerate, and slow. After dealing with a preliminary matter, that had been held over from the day before, the court clerk handed Judge Stephens the list of all those to be arraigned. There were at least forty of us in the room, most of whom were there for drunk driving.

For a full ten minutes, the judge, in a concerned manner, read us our various rights plus the court procedures. As Judge Stephens talked, I began to relax, my anxiety level dropped noticeably, all due, I'm sure, to the easy way of the soft-spoken man in the black robe.

The clerk read the names, and each person was required to answer "Here" and step up to the bailiff to receive three papers. The first was the criminal complaint, which spelled out the offence, "The criminal trespass-occupation." The charge read: that I

. . . did willfully and unlawfully commit a trespass by entering and occupying real property and a structure located at D and Mission Street, San Rafael, without the consent of the owner, his agent, and the person in lawful possession thereof, to Nance Philip Warren [not his real name].

The second paper was a list of thirteen "Rights of Defendants," and was essentially what Judge Stephens read at the outset. Reading the list of rights, it became clear to me that the arraignment was actually the equivalent of an arrest. Included in my rights was the right to a jury trial, if I pleaded not guilty and was released on bail.

I didn't like the sound of the latter. My intention was to represent myself. I'm one of the middle people. I make too much money to request a public defender, but I don't have the means to hire my own attorney. I'm forced to be my own lawyer.

The third paper, a brilliant orange in color, was a waiver form for persons who wanted to plead guilty and get the whole thing over as quickly as possible. Knowing the general leniency of the courts, I figured I could get off cheaply enough. However, I knew I was innocent, and I didn't want a criminal charge, even a misdemeanor, on my record. My intention was to fight the charge all the way through, even if it meant a jury trial.

After all the names were called and the papers distributed, Judge Stephens left the bench. The bailiff told me I should wait and talk to the judge. A half hour later, the judge reappeared and began calling out the names on the list—not all of them, but some. I couldn't figure out the procedure, but I was waiting for my name to be called.

The anxiety level was growing again, probably because I didn't know what was going on. The judge read my name, and I walked forward and stood behind the attorney's desk.

"Kent Allan Philpott, how do you plead?"

"Not guilty, your Honor."

"Do you want to waive time?"

"I don't understand, sir?'

Judge Stephens explained, but I still didn't understand.

"No, I don't want to waive time. I just want to have an opportunity to talk to the district attorney's office, hoping to get this matter dismissed."

"Your next court date then will be April 26 at 1:30 PM."

And that was it. I walked upstairs to the D.A.'s office to get a copy of the police report. From there, I went back to my office. Terry was at his desk, typing proofs of service.

He stopped his work as I sat down and put my feet on my desk.

"What happened?"

"Well, I was arraigned. No surprises. I pleaded not guilty and told Judge Stephens that I would represent myself. That was it. I got a copy of the police report and made an appointment with a Mary Pugalis, the expeditor in the D.A.'s office, as Steve Abbott said I should do. That's in two days."

"How do you feel?"

"I'd like to be a lot calmer than I am. Innocent or not, the fact of being charged with a crime is unsettling. Fortunately, I'm not terribly worried about what people will say; they usually think the worst anyway, but having your name called out in court is not a fun thing."

"The worst that can happen is a fine," Terry commented.

"There's no way I can pay a fine. I'd have to work it off some way."

"At $3.00 or so an hour, that might mean a long time. Doing it in jail would be cheaper, but we can't afford to have you gone."

"Terry, I can't see how this will go. I really think it'll be dismissed."

"I think you're right. You never know. But if it goes, you'd be better off with just a judge and not a jury."

"I thought I'd go for a jury trial. I can't see how a jury would convict me."

"You don't know those guys in the D.A.'s office. It's like a game with them, and winning is the only thing that counts. They don't care about justice. The D.A. will say, 'This guy makes his living serving legal papers on you and me. These guys have a reputation for serving a person any way they can.'"

"Yeah, I guess so."

"See, a judge will more likely make a decision on the evidence and the law. D.A.s don't."

"That makes sense, Terry, thanks. I'll go with a judge then."

Criminal trespass requires criminal intent. And I knew there was none. It was a simple serve, a small claims paper. The plaintiff had hired the defendant to repair her roof. She'd paid him, but the roof leaked. She filed on him in small claims and sent the paper to us to serve.

The defendant lived in a big old house in San Rafael. The plaintiff had given directions saying that the defendant lived in an apartment in the back and the stairs could be found in the back. At nine o'clock, February 17, I stopped at the address to make the serve. Locating the stairs in the rear, I climbed them and knocked on the door.

"Is Nance Warner here?"

"Knocking around here pretty late, aren't you?"

"You're right. Sorry."

"You're on the wrong stairs. Warner lives on the other side."

"Thanks. Sorry to bother you."

I couldn't find any other stairs. Around and around, I walked. The only possibility was to try the front door. The big glass front entrance was open. I found myself in a small dark entrance hallway with three doors leading off it. I knocked on all three. Nothing. A sign reading "STORAGE" was over one door, but two others were blank. I figured one door opened into a stairway, which would lead me to Warner's apartment.

The first door I tried was unlocked. I stepped inside and, before me was a flight of stairs. Before I could move a step, Nance Warner appeared at the top of the stairs. He looked about thirty, blonde hair, about 6'2", and he had no shirt on.

"How'd you get in here?"

"I just walked in. I'm a process server, and I'm looking for Nance Warner."

"I'm Nance Warner."

"I have a legal paper for you."

"Get out of here, you bastard."

"Okay, I'm gone." I let the small claims paper flutter to the floor and I stepped out the door into the hallway. Warner was right behind me, yelling and cursing and punching. He had me trapped. The entrance was so small that there was no room for me to maneuver in order to get out the front door.

Warner was in a rage. I could hear a woman wildly yelling for him to let me go. I made no effort to fight. I simply wanted out.

"Let me out; I just want out."

I edged to the door and opened it a crack, when Warner kicked me hard in the butt. The kick threw him off balance for an instant, and I got halfway out before he unleashed a vicious right round house that caught me on the neck. But I was out and once outside, I was ready to fight back. By then, though, Warner didn't want anymore.

Shaken and mad, I walked to a service station and called the police. An officer Sullivan showed up in a black and white and listened to my statement. He told me he'd talk to Warner and send a report to the district attorney's office. I wanted Warner charged with battery. Instead, Warner accused me of trespassing, saying he hit me to protect himself and his wife. He lied and said it all happened in his apartment. So, reading Sullivan's report, the D.A. said Warner had a right to hit me and I was guilty of a trespass.

At best, I had wandered into Warner's apartment by accident. Certainly, there was no criminal intent, and, as I believed the law worked, I would have to have had criminal intent. It seemed to me that the D.A. would dismiss the charge once I had a chance to explain things.

At worst, I was guilty of a misdemeanor with no previous record. That meant a fine and probation. The real cost, though, was the anxiety that I had to deal with and the time spent in rolling the mess over and over in my mind. And it slowed me down in my work, since I had to be extra careful that there were no other incidents. I could imagine what a genuinely serious charge could do to a person's life. For a high-strung person like me, the days spent waiting for the wheels of justice to grind brought me considerable discomfort. All I could do was to wait; I was not in control. The people of the State of California were going to have a go at me.

The wheels of justice sped up some. Two days after my arraignment, I met with a deputy district attorney who functioned as the "Expeditor." Her job was to clean up the system by whatever means possible. I knew beforehand that she had the authority to recommend my case be dismissed. Terry doubted whether I would be so fortunate and was expecting a tough uphill battle. But I was hopeful. Locked in me was the long-cherished belief that the legal system was basically fair. Knowing I was innocent, I couldn't imagine being convicted of any crime. As my nerves began to settle out, I figured the episode would serve well as a chapter in this book.

However, the final results leave this chapter a bit flat. The "expeditor," after listening to my story said,

"This should never have been filed on in the first place."

I remained silent.

"You're a process server; you were doing your job. You were even attacked. Nothing serious happened. No loss. No injury."

"It pleases me a great deal to hear you say that. The

last thing I wanted was a criminal record."

"Were you going to refile your complaint against Warner?"

"It was the worst attack on me ever. If I don't, he will have simply accomplished his purpose. But then, I feel like I've had enough of this. No, I'm going to let it go. The whole thing will at least serve as a good ending to my book on process serving."

"Oh, you're doing a book?"

"Working on it for nearly two years. And this will be it."

"Why'd you do it?"

"I like to write, and I felt there might be some interest in what process servers do. There's a lot of ordinary type life touched on, crucial kinds of things happening to people that I, for one, never realized."

"Don't use my name."

"Don't worry —I'll change everything around."